1932
HOPI AND NAVAJO
NATIVE AMERICAN CENSUS
WITH BIRTH & DEATH ROLLS
(1925 - 1931)
VOLUME 1 - HOPI

TRANSCRIBED BY
JEFF BOWEN
NATIVE STUDY
Gallipolis, Ohio
USA

Originally published:
Baltimore, Maryland
2013

Reprinted by:

Native Study LLC
Gallipolis, OH
www.nativestudy.com
2020

Library of Congress Control Number: 2020916727

ISBN: 978-1-64968-055-6

Made in the United States of America.

Other Books and Series by Jeff Bowen

1901-1907 Native American Census Seneca, Eastern Shawnee, Miami, Modoc, Ottawa, Peoria, Quapaw, and Wyandotte Indians (Under Seneca School, Indian Territory)

1932 Census of The Standing Rock Sioux Reservation with Births And Deaths 1924-1932

Census of The Blackfeet, Montana, 1897- 1901 Expanded Edition

Eastern Cherokee by Blood, 1906-1910, Volumes I thru XIII

Choctaw of Mississippi Indian Census 1929-1932 with Births and Deaths 1924-1931 Volume I

Choctaw of Mississippi Indian Census 1933, 1934 & 1937, Supplemental Rolls to 1934 & 1935 with Births and Deaths 1932-1938, and Marriages 1936-1938 Volume II

Eastern Cherokee Census Cherokee, North Carolina 1930-1939 Census 1930-1931 with Births And Deaths 1924-1931 Taken By Agent L. W. Page Volume I

Eastern Cherokee Census Cherokee, North Carolina 1930-1939 Census 1932-1933 with Births And Deaths 1930-1932 Taken By Agent R. L. Spalsbury Volume II

Eastern Cherokee Census Cherokee, North Carolina 1930-1939 Census 1934-1937 with Births and Deaths 1925-1938 and Marriages 1936 & 1938 Taken by Agents R. L. Spalsbury And Harold W. Foght Volume III

Seminole of Florida Indian Census, 1930-1940 with Birth and Death Records, 1930-1938

Texas Cherokees 1820-1839 A Document For Litigation 1921

Choctaw By Blood Enrollment Cards 1898-1914 Volumes I thru XVII

Starr Roll 1894 (Cherokee Payment Rolls) Districts: Canadian, Cooweescoowee, and Delaware Volume One

Starr Roll 1894 (Cherokee Payment Rolls) Districts: Flint, Going Snake, and Illinois Volume Two

Starr Roll 1894 (Cherokee Payment Rolls) Districts: Saline, Sequoyah, and Tahlequah; Including Orphan Roll Volume Three

Other Books and Series by Jeff Bowen

Cherokee Intruder Cases Dockets of Hearings 1901-1909 Volumes I & II

Indian Wills, 1911-1921 Records of the Bureau of Indian Affairs Books One thru Seven;

Native American Wills & Probate Records 1911-1921

Turtle Mountain Reservation Chippewa Indians 1932 Census with Births & Deaths, 1924-1932

Chickasaw By Blood Enrollment Cards 1898-1914 Volume I thru V

Cherokee Descendants East An Index to the Guion Miller Applications Volume I
Cherokee Descendants West An Index to the Guion Miller Applications Volume II (A-M)
Cherokee Descendants West An Index to the Guion Miller Applications Volume III (N-Z)

Applications for Enrollment of Seminole Newborn Freedmen, Act of 1905

Eastern Cherokee Census, Cherokee, North Carolina, 1915-1922, Taken by Agent James E. Henderson   *Volume I (1915-1916)*
Volume II (1917-1918)
Volume III (1919-1920)
Volume IV (1921-1922)

Complete Delaware Roll of 1898

Eastern Cherokee Census, Cherokee, North Carolina, 1923-1929, Taken by Agent James E. Henderson   *Volume I (1923-1924)*
Volume II (1925-1926)
Volume III (1927-1929)

Applications for Enrollment of Seminole Newborn Act of 1905 Volumes I & II

North Carolina Eastern Cherokee Indian Census 1898-1899, 1904, 1906, 1909-1912, 1914 Revised and Expanded Edition

Visit our website at **www.nativestudy.com** to learn more about these and other books and series by Jeff Bowen

This series is dedicated to the
Navajo and Hopi people.

TABLE OF CONTENTS

INTRODUCTION

This census was originally transcribed by this author in April 1997. The census was placed in two volumes because there was such a large difference involving the structure of yearly separations, as is evident from the table of contents for each volume. This work was obtained from National Archives microfilm M-595, Roll 192.

The Hopi Indians, are a divisional group of the Pueblo peoples from the Southwest cultural area. Living in northeastern Arizona they usually lived near high mesas or flat-topped hills with steep sides where they formed pueblos, small communities or villages that were self-governed.

Hopi people are known as diligent agriculturists as well as very talented artisans. The Hopi religion emphasizes worship of the forces of nature, and has many different ceremonies intended to invoke supernatural powers. A few of the more important Hopi religious ceremonies include: the Kachina Fertility mysteries as well as the Midsummer and Midwinter rituals of Sun and Fire worship. The most intense ceremony performed and celebrated by the Hopi people is the Snake dance which is staged every two years. They also practice the Kachina Dance as well as the Flute ceremony. They feel their people have a roll as caretakers of the earth.

As with most Native cultures the Hopi people have watched their culture change with the modernization of American life and population increase. From the 2010 publication, *Indian Nations of North America,* it states "Hopi people refer to their ancestors as Hisatsinom ("People of Long Ago"), while archaeologists refer to them as Anasazi or San Juan basketmakers. They formed small settlements in a region stretching from the Grand Canyon to Toko'navi (Navajo Mountain) in present-day Utah, eastward to the Lukachukai Mountains near the New Mexico-Arizona border, and south to the Mogollon Rim. Small masonry villages were built between 900 and 1100, but a severe, long-lasting drought forced the abandonment of 36 of the 47 mesa-top villages. Following the drought, the 11 remaining villages grew in size, and three more were developed. Thus, the modern-day Hopi have lived in the Black Mesa region of the Colorado Plateau for nearly 1,000 years. The Hopi village of Old Oraibi is considered one of the oldest continuously occupied cities in the United States.

"The Spanish visited the region several times between 1540 and the Pueblo Revolt in 1680. During the revolt, the Hopi moved many of their villages to mesa tops for defensive purposes and sheltered refugees from other pueblos."[1]

"The Hopi currently live in 13 villages on three thin mesas projecting south from Black Mesa and to the west along Moencopi Wash. Their homeland is called Tutsqua. Every village is relatively autonomous, but only one has adopted a constitution and established a westernized government--the 11 other villages operate with some degree of adherence to the traditional Hopi form of governance. Oraibi remains traditional."[2]

---

[1] National Geographic Indian Nations of North America p. 213-214.
[2] National Geographic Indian Nations of North America p. 214.

INTRODUCTION

The Navajo, also spelled Navaho, Indians of the Southwest also live on reservations in northeastern Arizona, while parts adjoin to both New Mexico and Utah. They originally called themselves Tinneh or the People, but with time they would be called Apache and Navajo by people they came in contact with. Their dialects were from the same Athapaskan decent. Their religion was simply founded on overseeing nature and healing the sick. Eventually, "Like any people spread out over a vast and variable landscape, they gradually splintered into distinct groups, which the Spaniards began to distinguish with separate names."[3] "Spread out along the northern borders of New Mexico and Arizona were the Apaches de Nabajo--later shorten to Navajo--who developed a far different way of life than the other groups."[4] In time they would become so different that they would identify themselves as the, Dine', The People. During the early times they began to live where the very ancient Anasazi lived. The Navajo became herdsmen, raising sheep and horses; Navajo women became weavers of the finest blankets. "In times of want, weaving often kept Navajo families alive. Woman sheared the sheep, and spun and dyed the wool, obtaining the soft hues from wild plants."[5]

Today the Navajo Reservation is the largest reservation in the United States; in fact, it is larger than the state of West Virginia.

"The tribe is a member of the Eight Northern Indian Pueblos Council, a nonprofit organization that provides community-based services to Nambė, Taos, Picuris, Ohkay Owingeh, Santa Clara, San Ildefonso, Pojoaque, and Tesuque Pueblos. The tribal economy is supported in large part from the tribe's agricultural enterprises."[6]

This two volume set contains a wealth of genealogical information that reveals the name, age at last birthday, marital status, degree of blood, relationship to Head of family, and in the case of the Hopi, the village the family was living at during the time of the census. The Birth and Death Rolls also contain valuable information like birth and death dates, the mother's and father's degree of blood, and in most cases the cause of death.

Jeff Bowen
Gallipolis, Ohio
NativeStudy.com

---

[3] The American Indians, People of The Desert p. 142.
[4] The American Indians, People of The Desert p. 142-145
[5] The American Indians, People of The Desert p. 166.
[6] Indian Nations of North America p. 224.

INSTRUCTIONS

(*A*) A separate roll is to be made of each reservation; also, of each *rancheria* or reserve, and a separate roll of Indians allotted on the public domain or homesteading. The roll is to be based on enrollment and not on residence.

(*B*) Persons are to be listed by families alphabetically; that is, not only by the first letter of the surname, but also by the second and subsequent letters when the first letter or letters are the same. For example: Ab*a*lon, Ab*b*ott, Ab*c*on, Ab*e*nd, Ab*i*ct; B*a*ll, B*e*ll, B*i*ll, B*o*ll, B*u*ll; ...etc. Families having the same surname are also to be listed in this way, e.g.; Brown, *A*nson; Brown, *B*ill; Brown, *C*harles; Brown, *D*avid. In the case of English translations of Indian names, such as John *Flying-Elk*, Flying-Elk is the surname and is to be listed under F. In such cases the first word of the translated Indian name determines the alphabetical position. The best way to accomplish this will be to write the names of each family group on a separate card; then, arrange the cards alphabetically and type the names therefrom onto the census roll.

Members of a family are to be listed in the following order: Head, first; wife, second; then children, whether sons or daughters, *in the order of their ages*; and lastly, all other relatives and persons living with the family who do not constitute another family group.

Annuity and per capita payment rolls are also to be prepared in the same manner.

(*C*) A family is composed of the following members:
1. Both parents and their unmarried children, if any, living with them; all other relatives and persons living with the family who do not constitute another family group.
2. Either parent and the unmarried children, if the other parent is dead; all other relatives and persons living with the family who do not constitute another family group.
3. A single person over 21 years of age, not living with a relative.

(*D*) For each person the following information is to be furnished:
1. NUMBER. – A number is to be assigned in serial order. Thus, the first person listed is to be numbered as "1," the second, as "2," and so on until the census is completed.
2. NAME. – If there are both an Indian and an English name, the allotment or annuity roll name is to be given. First, the last or surname; then, the given name in full. Ditto marks are to be used under the surname of the head for the surnames of the other members of one family.
3. SEX. – "M" for male; "F" for female.
4. AGE AT LAST BIRTHDAY. – Age in completed years at last birthday is to be shown. For infants under 1 year, age in

completed months, expressed as twelfths of a year. Thus, 3 months as 3/12 yr.

5. TRIBE. – Care is to be taken that tribe, not band or local name, is given. Thus, Ute tribe, not Pahvant, which is a band of Ute. Likewise, Hupa tribe, not Bear River, which is a local name for the members of the Hupa tribe living near Bear River.

6. DEGREE OF BLOOD. – "F" for full blood; "1/4+" for one-fourth or more Indian blood; "-1/4" for less than one fourth Indian blood.

7. MARITAL STATUS. – "S" for a single or unmarried person; "M" for a married person; and "W" for widowed of either sex.

8. RELATIONSHIP TO HEAD OF FAMILY. – The head, whether husband or father, widow or unmarried person of either sex, is to be designated as such. For the other members, the appropriate term which designates the particular relationship the person bears to the head is to be used.

9. RESIDENCE. –
   (a) At *jurisdiction* where enrolled: Yes or no. The term jurisdiction includes all reservations and public domain allotments under the agency.
   (b) *Or* at another jurisdiction. The name of the jurisdiction is to be given.
   (c) *Or* elsewhere:
      1. Post office: Both the proper name of the post office and the class by which it is known (city, town, village, etc.) are to be given. Thus, Lewiston, city.
      2. County.
      3. State.

10. WARD. – Yes or no. Wardship depends primarily upon the ownership of individual property held in trust or upon membership in a tribe living on a Federal reservation.

* 11. ALLOTMENT, ANNUITY, AND IDENTIFICATION NUMBERS. —"Al", for allotment; "An", for annuity; and "Id", for identification, before the appropriate number or numbers. All numbers are to be shown.

INSTRUCTIONS

** 11. (KEY TO VARIOUS HOPI VILLAGES). – Each letter
represents a different village, as follows:
A - Tewa
B - Sitchumnovi
C - Walpi
D - Mashongnovi
E - Chepaulovi
F - Chimopovy
G - Oraibi
H - Bacabi
I - Hotevilla

(E) Rolls not prepared in strict conformity with the above instructions will be
returned for correction.

*NOTE: These instructions are directed at the Navajo census ONLY.

**NOTE: These instructions are directed at the Hopi census ONLY

CENSUS

of the

HOPI TRIBE

Hopi Indian Reservation

of the

Hopi Indian Agency

Arizona Jurisdiction

HOPI INDIAN CENSUS, (As of April 1, 1932)

KEY: Census Number; Name; Sex; Age at Last Birthday; Tribe (Hopi, unless otherwise stated); Degree of Blood; Marital Status; Relationship to Head of Family; At Jurisdiction where enrolled [Yes or No] (If no, Where); Ward [Yes or No]; Hopi Village [according to key].

ACOYA

1; Henry; m; ?; F; m; Head; yes; yes; B
2; Frieda; f; 37 (1895); F; m; wife; yes; yes; B
3; Henry; m; 11 (1921); F; s; son; yes; yes; B
4; Alfred; m; 8 (1924); F; s; son; yes; yes; B
5; Dorothy; f; 6 (1926); F; s; dau; yes; yes; B

ADAMS

6; Byron; m; 41 (1891); F; m; Head; yes; yes; B
7; Sarah; f; 20 (1912); F; s; dau; yes; yes; B
8; Abbott; m; 18 (1914); F; s; son; yes; yes; B
9; Hazel; f; 16 (1916); F; s; dau; yes; yes; B

10; Gordon; m; 29 (1903); F; m; Head; yes; yes; B
11; Zilpah; f; 27 (1905); F; m; wife; yes; yes; B
12; Shirley; m; 8 (1924); F; s; son; yes; yes; B
13; Fern; f; 3 (12-9-28); F; s; dau; yes; yes; B
14; Roberta; f; 1 (9-11-30); F; s; dau; yes; yes; B

15; Orlin; m; 33 (1899); F; m; Head; yes; yes; C
16; Zella; f; 31 (1901); F; m; wife; yes; yes; C

17; Plinney; m; 39 (1893); F; m; Head; yes; yes; D
18; Ettie; f; 38 (1894); F; m; wife; yes; yes; D
19; Katherine; f; 19 (1913); F; s; dau; yes; yes; D
20; Richard Plinney; m; 11 (1921); F; s; son; yes; yes; D
21; Mae Thayer; f; 9 (1923); F; s; dau; yes; yes; D
22; Emily Ellen; f; 7 (1925); F; s; dau; yes; yes; D
23; Earl Anderson; m; 4 (2-28-28); F; s; son; yes; yes; D
24; Florence; f; 1 (9-13-30); F; s; Adpt dau; yes; yes; D

25; Wilbur; m; 34 (1898); F; m; Head; yes; yes; A
26; Sadie; f; 28 (1904); F; m; wife; yes; yes; A
27; Byron; m; 6 (2-12-26); F; s; son; yes; yes; A
28; Lorna; f; 2 (9-21-29); F; s; dau; yes; yes; A
29; Reba; f; 3/12 (12-16-31); F; s; dau; yes; yes; A

ADDINGTON

30; Charles; m; 33 (1899); F; m; Head; no; Pierre School, P.O. Pierre, Hughes Co, SD; yes; [village not given]

1

KEY: Census Number; Name; Sex; Age at Last Birthday; Tribe (Hopi, unless otherwise stated); Degree of Blood; Marital Status; Relationship to Head of Family; At Jurisdiction where enrolled [Yes or No] (If no, Where); Ward [Yes or No]; Hopi Village [according to key].

31; [**Mongue**], George K; m; 26 (1906); F; m; Head; yes; yes; G

32; [**Mahkewa**], Dorothy; f; 25 (1907); F; m; wife; yes; yes; G

ADKINSON

33; Dora; f; 41 (1891); F; w; Head; yes; yes; G

34; Thomas; m; 9 (1925); F; s; son; yes; yes; G

AHLONG

35; [Blank]; m; 61; (1871); F; m; Head; yes; yes; A

36. Nube; f; 60; (1872); F; m; wife; yes; yes; A

37; Mona Lee; f; 23 (1909); F; s; dau; yes; yes; A

38; Roy yo, Emily; f; 12 (1920); F; s; dau; yes; yes; A

AHME

39; Glenn; m; 31 (1901); F; m; Head; yes; yes; B

40; Nettie; f; 31 (1901); F; m; wife; yes; yes; B

41; Leroy; m; 10 (1922); F; s; son; yes; yes; B

42; Pearl; f; 7 (1925); F; s; dau; yes; yes; B

43; Alexander; m; 4 (2-1-28); F; s; son; yes; yes; B

44; Bettie; f; 1 (10-13-30); F; s; dau; yes; yes; B

45; [Blank]; m; 62 (1870); F; m; Head; yes; yes; B

46; Halmeta; f; 60 (1872); F; m; wife; yes; yes; B

47; Ira; m; 29 (1903); F; s; son; yes; yes; B

48; Kent; m; 22 (1910); F; s; son; yes; yes; B

49; Imes; m; 19 (1913); F; s; son; yes; yes; B

50; Clyde; m; 17 (1915); F; s; son; yes; yes; B

51; Nancy; f; 14 (1918); F; s; dau; yes; yes; B

AHOWANA

52; Jacob; m; 26 (1906); F; m; Head; yes; yes; H

53; Clara; f; ?; F; m; wife; yes; yes; H

54; Anita; f; 3 (1929); F; s; dau; yes; yes; H

55; Thomas; m; 1; (2-3-31); F; s; son; yes; yes; H

AHVATZHOIYA

56; Willie; m; 38 (1894); F; m; Head; yes; yes; B

57; Faye; f; 38 (1894); F; m; wife; yes; yes; B

58; Ruby; f; 11 (1921); F; s; dau; yes; yes; B

KEY: Census Number; Name; Sex; Age at Last Birthday; Tribe (Hopi, unless otherwise stated); Degree of Blood; Marital Status; Relationship to Head of Family; At Jurisdiction where enrolled [Yes or No] (If no, Where); Ward [Yes or No]; Hopi Village [according to key].

59; Bradford; m; 9 (1923); F; s; son; yes; yes; B

AHVIYO

60; Charley; m; 64 (1868); F; m; Head; yes; yes; A
61; Ahvotsa; f; 59 (1873); F; m; wife; yes; yes; A
62; Corrine; f; 19 (1913); F; s; dau; yes; yes; A

AHWACHOWA

63; Alice; f; 41 (1891); F; w; Head; yes; yes; A
64; Clarence; m; 21 (1911); F; s; son; yes; yes; A

ALBERT

65; Earl; m; 32 (1900); F; m; Head; yes; yes; I
66; Elizabeth; f; 26 (1906); F; m; wife; yes; yes; I
67; Myra; f; 6 (1926); F; s; dau; yes; yes; I
68; Romane; m; 4 (1928); F; s; son; yes; yes; I
69; Lynn; m; 2 (8-1-29); F; s; son; yes; yes; I
70; Pearl; f; 2/12 (1-5-32); F; s; dau; yes; yes; I

71; Walter; m; 31 (1901); F; m; Head; yes; yes; I
72; Martha; f; 24 (1908); F; m; wife; yes; yes; I

ANGAH

73; Preston; m; 61 (1871); F; m; Head; yes; yes; A
74; Talahvenice; f; 60 (1872); F; m; wife; yes; yes; A
75; Collins; m; 41 (1891); F; s; son; yes; yes; A
76; Ross; m; 19 (1913); F; s; son; yes; yes; A
77; Preston, Jr; m; 17 (1915); F; s; son; yes; yes; A

BACKAVIA

78; [Blank]; m; 63 (1869); F; w; Head; yes; yes; G

BACON

79; Susie; f; 56 (1876); F; w; Head; yes; yes; G
80; Suzanna; f; 17 (1915); F; s; stp-dau; yes; yes; G

3

HOPI INDIAN CENSUS, (As of April 1, 1932)

KEY: Census Number; Name; Sex; Age at Last Birthday; Tribe (Hopi, unless otherwise stated); Degree of Blood; Marital Status; Relationship to Head of Family; At Jurisdiction where enrolled [Yes or No] (If no, Where); Ward [Yes or No]; Hopi Village [according to key].

BAHNIMTIWA

81; [Blank]; m; ?; F; m; Head; yes; yes; G
82; Masameiam; f; 56 (1874); F; m; wife; yes; yes; G
83; Talashoynom; f; 26 (1906); F; s; dau; yes; yes; G
84; Tuwanomsi; f; 22 (1910); F; s; dau; yes; yes; G
85; Fern; f; 20 (1912); F; s; dau; yes; yes; G
86; Lilah; f; 18 (1914); F; s; dau; yes; yes; G
87; Stanley; m; 12; (1920); F; s; son; yes; yes; G

BATALA

88; Theodore; m; 38 (1894); F; m; Head; yes; yes; D
89; (Ciichwesnema), Esther; f; 35 (1897); F; m; wife; yes; yes; D
90; Charlotte; f; 16 (1916); F; s; dau; yes; yes; D
91; Jane; f; 14 (1918); F; s; dau; yes; yes; D
92; Stewart; m; 10 (1822); F; s; son; yes; yes; D
93; Virginia; f; 8 (1924); F; s; dau; yes; yes; D
94; Emil; m; 6 (11-3-26); F; s; son; yes; yes; D
95; Percy; m; 2 (8-13-29); F; s; son; yes; yes; D
96; Tenny; m; 5/12 (10-12-31); F; s; son; yes; yes; D

BATANHOYA

97; Cecil Calvert; m; 29 (1903); F; m; Head; yes; yes; D
98; (Watkins), Flora Mae; f; 26 (1906); F; m; wife; yes; yes; D
99; **Watkins**, Russel; m; 4 (1928); F; s; stp-son; yes; yes; D
100; Leonora M; f; 1 (6-26-30); F; s; dau; yes; yes; D

BONEY

101; Donald; m; 44 (1889); F; m; Head; yes; yes; G
102; Mary; f; 44 (1889); F; m; wife; yes; yes; G
103; Ernest; m; 22 (1919); F; s; son; yes; yes; G
104; Carl; m; 20 (1912); F; s; son; yes; yes; G
105; Myrtle; f; 15 (1917); F; s; dau; yes; yes; G
106; Alma; f; 9 (1923); F; s; dau; yes; yes; G
107; Edman; m; 7 (1925); F; s; son; yes; yes; G

BOZURKA

108; Milton; m; 30 (1902); F; m; Head; yes; yes; E
109; (Cashwonka), Agnes; f; 27 (1905); F; m; wife; yes; yes; E
110; **Numkewa**, Thelma; f; 9 (1923); F; s; dau; yes; yes; E

HOPI INDIAN CENSUS, (As of April 1, 1932)

KEY: Census Number; Name; Sex; Age at Last Birthday; Tribe (Hopi, unless otherwise stated); Degree of Blood; Marital Status; Relationship to Head of Family; At Jurisdiction where enrolled [Yes or No] (If no, Where); Ward [Yes or No]; Hopi Village [according to key].

111; Margarita; f; 3 (1029); F; s; dau; yes; yes; E

CALOMYTIWA

112; Cecil; m; 25 (1907); F; m; Head; yes; yes; G
113; (Kuwanventewa), Juanita; f; 21 (1911); F; m; wife; yes; yes; G
114; Patsy Anne; f; 1/12 (2-16-32); F; s; dau; yes; yes; G

CALETSONG

115; [Blank]; f; 59 (1875); F; w; Head; yes; yes; A

CARL

116; Edwin F; m; 54 (1878); F; m; Head; yes; yes; A
117; Hattie; f; 50 (1882); F; m; wife; yes; yes; A
118; Ralph Collins; m; 17 (1915); F; s; son; yes; yes; A
119; Jennie; f; 15 (1917); F; s; dau; yes; yes; A

CHAKA

120; Harry; m; 24 (1908); F; m; Head; yes; yes; B
121; (Pavatea), Airlie; f; 20 (1912); F; m; wife; yes; yes; B

122; Joseph; m; 26 (1906); F; w; Head; yes; yes; A
123; Nellie; f; 3 (11-28-28); F; s; dau; yes; yes; A

124; Oilver[sic]; m; 55 (1877); F; w; Head; yes; yes; A

125; Charley; m; 70 (1862); F; w; Head; yes; yes; B

CHEEDA

126; Hicks; m; 42 (1890); F; s; Head; yes; yes; B

CHEEOUMA

127; Newton; m; 48 (1884); F; w; Head; yes; yes; C
128; Francis; m; 16 (1916); F; s; son; yes; yes; C
129; Mark; m; 14 (1918); F; s; son; yes; yes; C

CHEKUMIA

130; James; m; 33 (1899); F; m; Head; yes; yes; H

5

HOPI INDIAN CENSUS, (As of April 1, 1932)

KEY: Census Number; Name; Sex; Age at Last Birthday; Tribe (Hopi, unless otherwise stated); Degree of Blood; Marital Status; Relationship to Head of Family; At Jurisdiction where enrolled [Yes or No] (If no, Where); Ward [Yes or No]; Hopi Village [according to key].

131; Frances; f; 33 (1899); F; m; wife; yes; yes; H
132; Paul; m; 22 (1921); F; s; son; yes; yes; H
133; Laura; f; 9 (1923); F; s; dau; yes; yes; H
134; Forrest; m; 6 (1926); F; s; son; yes; yes; H
135; Burke; m; 4 (10-1-27); F; s; son; yes; yes; H
136; Nona; f; 2 (2-15-30); f; S; dau; yes; yes; H
137; Leonora; f; 1/12 (3-3-32); F; s; dau; yes; yes; H

CHICUOOMA

138; Henry; m; 39 (1893); F; m; Head; yes; yes; I
139; Lydia; f; 38 (1894); F; m; wife; yes; yes; I
140; Ida Mae; f; 10 (1922); F; s; dau; yes; yes; I
141; Martha; f; 8 (1924); F; s; dau; yes; yes; I
142; Donald; m; 2 (11-5-29); F; s; son; yes; yes; I
143; Wesley; m; 612 (9-30-31); F s; son; yes; yes; I

CHORO

144; Stuart; m; 31 (1901); F; m; Head; yes; yes; C
145; Ida Martin; f; 21 (1911); F; m; wife; yes; yes; C

146; [Blank]; m; 75 (1857); F; w; Head; yes; yes; E

CHOROVOHO

147; Jerry; m; 48 (1884); F; m; Head; yes; yes; E
148; (Kowanvensic), Sophie; f; 50 (1882); F; m; wife; yes; yes; E
149; **Poneoma**, Wesley; m; 24; (1908); F; s; son; yes; yes; E
150; Bert; m; 15 (1917); F; s; son; yes; yes; E
151; Mary May; f; 7 (1925); F; s; dau; yes; yes; E
152; **Queyesnema**, Lillian; f; 19 (1913); F; s; stp-dau; yes; yes; E
153; **Queyesnema**, Lorena; f; 1/12 (3-10-32); F; s; stp grand-dau; yes; yes; E
154; **Eptavi**, Beatrice; f; 10 (1922); F; s; stp-dau; yes; yes; E

CHOSEHOUNCIE

155; [Blank]; m; 42 (1884); F; w; Head; yes; yes; I
156; Viness; m; 16 (1916); F; s; son; yes; yes; I
157; Hughes; m; 12 (1920); F; s; son; yes; yes; I

CHOOSEMAESE

158; [Blank]; m; 49 (1883); F; w; Head; yes; yes; I

KEY: Census Number; Name; Sex; Age at Last Birthday; Tribe (Hopi, unless otherwise stated); Degree of Blood; Marital Status; Relationship to Head of Family; At Jurisdiction where enrolled [Yes or No] (If no, Where); Ward [Yes or No]; Hopi Village [according to key].

159; Charley; m; 18 (1914); F; s; son; yes; yes; I
160; Joe; m; 15 (1917); F; s; son; yes; yes; I
161; Saul; m; 10 (1922); F; s; son; yes; yes; I
162; De Alva; f; 6 (1926); F; s; dau; yes; yes; I

CHOWATTIE

163; James; m; 35 (1897); F; s; Head; yes; yes; B

CHOYHOYOKI

164; Reuben; m; 27 (1905); F; m; Head; yes; yes; I
165; Hester; f; 25 (1909); F; m; wife; yes; yes; I
166; Frank; m; 4 (3-31-28); F; s; son; yes; yes; I
167; Conner; m; 4/12 (11-12-31); f; s; son; yes; yes; I

CHUAHNUMPTOWA

168; Matthew; m; 26 (1906); F; m; Head; yes; yes; I
169; Hannah; f; 24 (1908); F; m; wife; yes; yes; I
170; Melvin; m; 1/12 (3-13-32); F; s; son; yes; yes; I

CHUAHONGIMA

171; James; m; 31 (1901); F; m; Head; yes; yes; I
172; Florence; f; 27 (1905); F; m; wife; yes; yes; I
173; Isabel; f; 9 (1923); F; s; dau; yes; yes; I
174; Inas; f; 5 (3-20-27(; F; s; dau; yes; yes; I
175; Amy; f; 1 (1930); F; s; dau; yes; yes; I

CHUAHYOUMA

176; Gus; m; 38 (1894); F; m; Head; yes; yes; A
177; Anna Belle; f; 31 (1901); F; m; wife; yes; yes; A
178; Alice; f; 11 (1931); F; s; dau; yes; yes; A
179; Norma; m; 7 (1925); F; s; son; yes; yes; A
180; Lois Evelyn; f; 1 (8-20-30); F; s; dau; yes; yes; A

CHUKA

181; Don; m; 40 (1892); F; m; Head; yes; yes; G
182; Irene; f; 40 (1892); F; m; wife; yes; yes; G

KEY: Census Number; Name; Sex; Age at Last Birthday; Tribe (Hopi, unless otherwise stated); Degree of Blood; Marital Status; Relationship to Head of Family; At Jurisdiction where enrolled [Yes or No] (If no, Where); Ward [Yes or No]; Hopi Village [according to key].

CHUKAHHOYA

183; [Blank]; m; 81 (1851); F; m; Head; yes; yes; G
184; [Blank]; f; 74 (1858); F; m; wife; yes; yes; G

CHUWWANCY

185; Bennett; m; 30 (1902); F; m; Head; yes; yes; A
186; Kewahne; f; 26 (1906); F; m; wife; yes; yes; A
187; Laverne; f; 6 (1926); F; s; dau; yes; yes; A
188; Constance; f; 4 (4-13-28); F; s; dau; yes; yes; A
189; **Betarooshie**, Phillip; m; 25 (1907); F; s; bro; yes; yes; A

CHUYOU

190; [Blank]; m; 55 (1877); F; m; Head; yes; yes; A
191; Hellen; f; 41 (1891); F; m; wife; yes; yes; A
192; Edwin Carl; m; 8 (1924); F; s; son; yes; yes; A

COCHYTEWA

193; Hugh; m; 37 (1895); F; m; Head; yes; yes; F
194; Emma; f; 36 (1898); F; m; wife; yes; yes; F
195; Wayne; m; 18 (1914); F; s; son; yes; yes; F
196; Kenneth; m; 15; F; s; son; yes; yes; F

COIN

197; Jacob; m; 57 (1875); F; m; Head; yes; yes; G
198; Bessie; f; 48 (1884); F; m; wife; yes; yes; G
199; Willie; m; 25 (1907); F; s; son; yes; yes; G
200; Felix; m; 17 (1915); F; s; son; yes; yes; G
201; Elenore; f; 13 (1919); F; s; dau; yes; yes; G
202; Pauline; f; 11 (1921); F; s; dau; yes; yes; G
203; Nina Marie; f; 2 (1930); F; s; dau; yes; yes; G

COLLATOTA

204; Morris; m; 28 (1904); F; m; Head;yes;yes;A
205; Madge; f; 22 (1910); F; m; wife; yes; yes; A

COMAHLETZTEWA

206; [Blank]; m; 54 (1878); F; m; Head; yes; yes; I

8

KEY: Census Number; Name; Sex; Age at Last Birthday; Tribe (Hopi, unless otherwise stated); Degree of Blood; Marital Status; Relationship to Head of Family; At Jurisdiction where enrolled [Yes or No] (If no, Where); Ward [Yes or No]; Hopi Village [according to key].

207; Dyoyemin; f; 54 (1878); F; m; wife; yes; yes; I
208; Abagail; f; 17 (1915); F; s; dau; yes; yes; I
209; Rodger; m; 15 (1917); F; s; son; yes; yes; I

CONGEYAH

210; [Blank]; f; 75 (1857); F; w; Head; yes; yes; C

COOCHESNEMA

211; Jessie; f; 51 (1881); F; s; Head; yes; yes; E
212; **Hoskie**, Victor; m; 27 (1905); F; s; nephew; yes; yes; E

COOCHISE

213; George; m; 53 (1879); F; m; Head; yes; yes; B
214; Lucy; f; 52 (1889); F; m; wife; yes; yes; B
215; Jacob Breed; m; 17 (1915); F; s; son; yes; yes; B

COOCHMANOMA

216; [Blank]; f; 59 (1873); F; w; Head; yes; yes; D
217; **Tuvacivia**, Scott; m; 27 (1905); F; s; son; yes; yes; D

COOCHQUAFTEWA

218; [Blank]; m; 60 (1872); F; w; Head; yes; yes; D

COOCHWYTEWA

219; Edward; m; 46 (1886); F; m; Head; yes; yes; D
220; (Coochquafnema), Beulah; f; 46 (1886); F; m; wife; yes; yes; D
221; **Masquafnma**, Ruth; f; 19 (1913); F; s; dau; yes; yes; D
222; **Kaloctaca**, Bruce; m; 18 (1914); F; s; son; yes; yes; D
223; **Ponyatskooma**, Moody; m; 13 (1919); F; s; son; yes; yes; D
224; Douglas; m; 9 (1923); F; s; son; yes; yes; D
225; **Kweanverzuh**, [Blank]; m; 60 (1872); F; w; uncle; yes; yes; D
226; **Coochhaftewa**, Guy; 43 (1889); F; w; cou; yes; yes; D

COOCHYOUMA

227; William; m; 36 (1896); F; m; Head; yes; yes; B
228; Matilda; f; 35 (1897); F; m; wife; yes; yes; B
229; Patrick; m; 13 (1919); F; s; son; yes; yes; B

9

KEY: Census Number; Name; Sex; Age at Last Birthday; Tribe (Hopi, unless otherwise stated); Degree of Blood; Marital Status; Relationship to Head of Family; At Jurisdiction where enrolled [Yes or No] (If no, Where); Ward [Yes or No]; Hopi Village [according to key].

230; Nana; f; 11 (1921); F; s; dau; yes; yes; B
231; Sanford; m; 6 (3-14-26); F; s; son; yes; yes; B
232; Mathius; m; 3 (6-30-28); F; s; son; yes; yes; B
233; Geneva; 9/12 (6-20-31); F; s; dau; yes; yes; B

COTISITEWA

234; Franklin; m; 58 (1874); F; m; Head; yes; yes; F
235; Mary; f; 56 (1876); F; m; wife; yes; yes; F
236; **Honewheuma**, Samuel; m; 54 (1878); F; w; bro-in-law; yes; yes; F

DAHO

237; Roy; m; 29 (1903); F; m; Head; yes; yes; B
238. Elinore; f; 28 (1904); F; m; wife; yes; yes; B

239; [Blank]; m; 64 (1868); F; m; Head; yes; yes; B
240; Kocyobbe; f; 63 (1869); F; m; wife; yes; yes; B
241; Logan; m; 29 (1903); F; s; son; yes; yes; B
242; Maxine; f; 22 (1910); F; s; dau; yes; yes; B
243; George; m; 20 (1912); F; s; son; yes; yes; B

DAHQUI

244; Edwin; m; 65 (1867); F; m; Head; yes; yes; B
245; Nina; F; 65 (1867); F; m; wife; yes; yes; B
246; Millicent; f; 12 (1920); F; s; dau; yes; yes; B
247; Bessie; f; 10 (1922); F; s; dau; yes; yes; B

DASH

248; Stanley; m; 23 (1909); F; m; Head; yes; yes; I
249; Marion; f; 21 (1911); F; m; wife; yes; yes; I
250; Muriel; f; 10/12 (5-2-31); F; s; dau; yes; yes; I

DASHEE

251; Stanley; m; 30 (1902); F; m; Head; yes; yes; A
252; Mabel; f; 26 (1906); F; m; wife; yes; yes; A
253; Anita; f; 7 (1925); F; s; dau; yes; yes; A
254; Loraine; f; 2 (4-20-30); F; s; dau; yes; yes; A
255; Caroline Lenora; f; 3/12 (12-29-31); F; s; dau; yes; yes; A

KEY: Census Number; Name; Sex; Age at Last Birthday; Tribe (Hopi, unless otherwise stated); Degree of Blood; Marital Status; Relationship to Head of Family; At Jurisdiction where enrolled [Yes or No] (If no, Where); Ward [Yes or No]; Hopi Village [according to key].

256; [Blank]; m; 65 (1869); F; m; Head; yes; yes; B
257; Harriet; f; 61 (1871); F; m; wife; yes; yes; B
258; Willie; m; 41 (1891); F; s; son; yes; yes; B
259; Meloin; m; 19 (1913); F; s; son; yes; yes; B

DAUNGEVA

260; Joe; m; 40 (1892); F; m; Head; yes; yes; F
261; Gay; f; 31 (1901); F; m; wife; yes; yes; F
262; Laura; f; 10 (1922); F; s; dau; yes; yes; F
263; Saral f; 3 (2-5-29); F; s; dau; yes; yes; F

DAVID

264; Abbott K; m; 30 (1902); F; m; Head; yes; yes; C
265; Janet; f; 26 (1906); F; m; wife; yes; yes; C
266; Ethel Ryan; f; 2 (7-7-29); F; s; dau; yes; yes; C
267; Gorman; m; 4/12 (11-14-31); F; s; son; yes; yes; C

DENEBE

268; Luther; m; 38 (1894); F; w; Head; yes; yes; G

DEWAHE

269; Don; m; 37 (1895); F; m; Head; yes; yes; H
270; Lucy; f; 34 (1898); F; m; wife; yes; yes; H
271; Orin; m; 9 (1923); F; s; son; yes; yes; H

DEWITT

272; Sahu; m; 33 (1899); F; m; Head; yes; yes; G
273; Ella; f; 28 (1904); F; m; wife; yes; yes; G
274; Sarah; f; 9 (1923); F; s; dau; yes; yes; G
275; David; m; 5 (11-7-26); F; s; son; yes; yes; G
276; Frances; f; 1 (12-11-30); F; s; dau; yes; yes; G

DINGAHVE

277; [Blank]; m; 60 (1872); F; w; Head; yes; yes; B

DIWAVENTHKA

278; [Blank]; f; 88 (1844); F; w; Head; yes; yes; F

11

HOPI INDIAN CENSUS, (As of April 1, 1932)

KEY: Census Number; Name; Sex; Age at Last Birthday; Tribe (Hopi, unless otherwise stated); Degree of Blood; Marital Status; Relationship to Head of Family; At Jurisdiction where enrolled [Yes or No] (If no, Where); Ward [Yes or No]; Hopi Village [according to key].

DOUMA

279; Douglas; m; 41 (1891); F; m; Head; yes; yes; A
280; Nellie; f; 36 (1896); F; m; wife; yes; yes; A
281; Marie; f; 18 (1914); F s; dau; yes; yes; A
282; Eloise; f; 16 (1916); F; s; dau; yes; yes; A
283; Augusta; f; 11 (1921); F; s; dau; yes; yes; A
284; Clara Lucille; f; 9 (1923); F; s; dau; yes; yes; A
285; Vernon; m; 6 (1926); F; s; son; yes; yes; A
286; Lindberg; m; 3 (12-5-28); F; s; son; yes; yes; A
287; Zella; f; 1 (10-1-30) F; s; dau; yes; yes; A

DEWAHOYA

288; Shirley; m; 36 (1896); F; m; Head; yes; yes; F
289; Eunice; f; 26 (1906); F; m; wife; yes; yes; F
290; Della; f; 7 (1925); F; s; dau; yes; yes; F
291; Thomas H; m; 4 (10-11-27); F; s; son; yes; yes; F

DUAHKPOO

292; [Blank]; m; 81 (1851); F; m; Head; yes; yes; C
293; Sunwyee; f; 66 (1866); F; m; wife; yes; yes; C
294; Tad; m; 26 (1906); F; s; son; yes; yes; C
295; Vera; f; 24 (1908); F; s; dau; yes; yes; C
296; Anthony; m; 19 (1913); F; s; son; yes; yes; C

DUERCHE

297; Tweitsie; m; 49 (1883); F; m; Head; yes; yes; C
298; Hattie; f; 47 (1886); F; m; wife; yes; yes; C
299; Dorothy; f; 30 (1902); F; s; dau; yes; yes; C
300; Leonard; m; 25 (1907); F; s; son; yes; yes; C
301; Christine; f; 24 (1908); F; s; dau; yes; yes; C
302; Hansen; m; 19 (1913); F; s; son; yes; yes; C
303; Isaac; m; 16 (1916); F; s; son; yes; yes; C
304; Elizabeth; f; 14 (1918); F; s; dau; yes; yes; C
305; Leita Grace; f; 10 (1922); F; s; dau; yes; yes; C
306; Myrtle Irene; f; 8 (1924); F; s; dau; yes; yes; C

DUERINGIVH

307; Cyrus; m; 42 (1890); F; w; Head; yes; yes; B
308; Byron; m; 16 (1916); F; s; son; yes; yes; B

309; Clark; m; 15 (1917); D: a; son; yes; yes; B
310; Rhomelda; f; 10 (1922); F; s; dau; yes; yes; B
311; Laurie; m; 8 (1924); F; s; son; yes; yes; B

DURVAHONGOVA

312; [Blank]; m; 49 (1883); F; m; Head; yes; yes; I
313; Naeninim; f; 49 (1883); F; m; wife; yes; yes; I
314; Emil; m; 20 (1912); F; s; son; yes; yes; I
315; Horace; m; 19 (1913); F; s; son; yes; yes; I
316; Vincent; m; 12 (1920); F; s; son; yes; yes; I
317; Edith; f; 1 (7-5-30); F; s; dau yes; yes; I

DUWAKUKU

318; George; m; 25 (1907); F; m; Head; yes; yes; A
319; Angella; f; 19 (1913); F; m; wife; yes; yes; A
320; George, Jr; m; 2 (4-17-29); F; s; son; yes; yes; A

321; [Blank]; m; 62 (1870); F; w; Head; yes; yes; A
322; Eugene; m; 21 (1911); F; s; son; yes; yes; A
323; Garnet; f; 17 (1915); F; s; dau; yes; yes; A

DUWYENIE

324; Andrew; m; 32 (1900); F; m; Head; yes; yes; I
325; Sarah; f; 30 (1902); F; m; wife; yes; yes; I
326; Junior; m; 12 (1920); F; s; son; yes; yes; I
327; Ronald; m; 10 (1922); F; s; son; yes; yes; I
328; Winston; m; 5 (2-24-27); F; s; son; yes; yes; I
329; Hubbell; m; 3 (1930); F; s; son; yes; yes; I

DUWYYOUMA

330; [Blank]; m; 66 (1866); F; w; Head; yes; yes; A
331; Pooya; m; 47 (1885); F; w; son; yes; yes; A

EAH

332; [Blank]; f; 65 (1869); F; w; Head; yes; yes; A
333; Taft; m; 25 (1907); F; s; son; yes; yes; A

HOPI INDIAN CENSUS, (As of April 1, 1932)

KEY: Census Number; Name; Sex; Age at Last Birthday; Tribe (Hopi, unless otherwise stated); Degree of Blood; Marital Status; Relationship to Head of Family; At Jurisdiction where enrolled [Yes or No] (If no, Where); Ward [Yes or No]; Hopi Village [according to key].

EVEHEMA

334; Dan; m; 32 (1900); F; m; Head; yes; yes; I
335; Isabel; f; 25 (1907); F; m; wife; yes; yes; I

FREDRICK

336; Charles; m; 53 (1879); F; m; Head; yes; yes; G
337; Anna; f; 45 (1998); F; m; wife; yes; yes; G
338; Oswald; m; 27 (1905); F; s; son; yes; yes; G
339; Jean; m; 25 (1907); F; s; son; yes; yes; G
340; Hulda; f; 26 (2908); F; s; dau; yes; yes; G
341; Margaret; F; 22 (1910); F; s; dau; yes; yes; G
342; Ida; f; 17 (1915); F; s; dau; yes; yes; G
343; Charlotte; f; 10 (1921); F; s; dau; yes; yes; G
344; Nathaniel; m; 8 (1924); F; s; son; yes; yes; G
345; John; m; 3 (5-20-28); F; s; son; yes; yes; G

346; Monroe; m; 44 (1889); F; m; Head; yes; yes; G
347; Nellie; f; 24 (1908); F; m; wife; yes; yes; G

348; Sequi James; m; 55 (1877); F; m; Head; yes; yes; G
349; Stella; f; 30 (1902); F; m; wife; yes; yes; G
350; Elizabeth; f; 12 (1920); F; s; dau; yes; yes; G
351; Stephen; m; 9 (1923); F; s; son; yes; yes; G
352; Jacob; m; 6 (1926); F; s; son; yes; yes; G
353; Marion; f; 3 (6-17-1928); F; s; dau; yes; yes; G
354; Roy; m; 8/12 (7-12-31); F; s; son; yes; yes; G

GAHLAH

355; Clifton; m; 43 (1889); F; m; Head; yes; yes; B
356; Una; f; 37 (1895); F; m; wife; yes; yes; B
357; Haysee; m; 22 (1910); F; s; son; yes; yes; B
358; Salome; f; 20 (1912); F; s; dau; yes; yes; B
359; Kathryn; f; 17 (1915); F; s; dau; yes; yes; B
360; Martha; f; 16 (1916); F; s; dau; yes; yes; B
361; Phoebe; f; 13 (1919); F; s; dau; yes; yes; B
362; Harout Ray; m; 11 (1921); F; s; son; yes; yes; B
363; Mary Bloomer; f; 9 (1923); F; s; dau; yes; yes; B
364; Alice Coleman; f; 7 (1925); F; s; dau; yes; yes; B
365; Phyllis; f; 4 (9-25-27); F; s; dau; yes; yes; B
366; Juanita; f; 2 (1929); F; s; dau; yes; yes; B
367; (Sahloe), [Blank]; f; 62 (1870); F; w; mother; yes; yes; B

14

HOPI INDIAN CENSUS, (As of April 1, 1932)

KEY: Census Number; Name; Sex; Age at Last Birthday; Tribe (Hopi, unless otherwise stated); Degree of Blood; Marital Status; Relationship to Head of Family; At Jurisdiction where enrolled [Yes or No] (If no, Where); Ward [Yes or No]; Hopi Village [according to key].

GAHOUTUH

368; [Blank]; m; 60 (1872); F; m; Head; yes; yes; A
369; Chongwa; f; 59 (1873); F; m; wife; yes; yes; A
370; Arthur; m; 33 (1899); F; s; son; yes; yes; A
371; Grant; m; 30 (1902); F; s; son; yes; yes; A
372; Rona; f; 21 (1911); F; s; dau; yes; yes; A

GASHNEYTEWA

373; [BLANK]; M; 84 (1848); F; w; Head; yes; yes; I

GASHWESEEMA

374; Frank; m; 40 (1898); F; m; Head; yes; yes; I
375; Le; f; 35 (1897); F; m; wife; yes; yes; I
376; Bryan; m; 15 (1917); F; s; son; yes; yes; I
377; Mamie; f; 13 (1919); F; s; dau; yes; yes; I
378; Lorenzo; m; 11 (1921); F; s; son; yes; yes; I
379; Martin; m; 9 (1923); F; s; son; yes; yes; I

GASHWYTEWA

380; [Blank]; m; 54 (1878); F; m; Head; yes; yes; I
381; Sewaquapnim; f; ? (1883); F; m; wife; yes; yes; I
382; Leon; m; 21 (1911); F; s; son; yes; yes; I
383; Lola; f; 18 (1914); F; s; dau; yes; yes; I
384; Ivan; m; 10 (1922); F; s; son; yes; yes; I

385; Jonathan; m; 26 (1906); F; m; Head; yes; yes; I
386; Nancy; f; 26 (1906); F; m; wife; yes; yes; I
387; Earl; m; 2 (6-23-29); F; s; son; yes; yes; I
388; Nancy Pauline; f; 7 (1925); F; s; stp-dau; yes; yes; I

GAYHE

389; [Blank];m; 56(1876); F; m; Head; yes;yes; I
390; Annuh; f; 45 (1887); F; m; wife; yes; yes; C
391; **Mahwah**, David; m; 28 (1905); F; s; son; yes; yes; C
392; Nancy; f; 12 (1920); F; s; dau; yes; yes; C
393; Bertha; f; 6 (1926); F; s; dau; yes; yes; C

15

KEY: Census Number; Name; Sex; Age at Last Birthday; Tribe (Hopi, unless otherwise stated); Degree of Blood; Marital Status; Relationship to Head of Family; At Jurisdiction where enrolled [Yes or No] (If no, Where); Ward [Yes or No]; Hopi Village [according to key].

GEASHONGAVA

394; [Blank]; f; 81 (1851); F; w; Head; yes; yes; F

GNEISIE

395; [Blank]; f; 84 (1848); F; w; Head; yes; yes; E
396; **Sequaftewa**, Rex; m; 31 (1901); F; m; gr-son; no; San Juan, P.O. Chamita Village, Rio Arriva, MN; yes; [village not given]
397; **Bayownema**, Ivie; f; 22 (1910); F; s; gr-dau; yes; yes; E
398; **Suanya**, Peter; m; 19 (1913); F; s; gr-son; yes; yes; E

GOOTA

399; Russell; m; 35 (1897); F; m Head; yes; yes; A
400; Edna; f; 36 (1896); F; m; wife; yes; yes; A
401; Elizabeth; f; 11 (1921); F; s; dau; yes; yes; A
402; Kathleen; f; 8 (1924); F; s; dau; yes; yes; A
403; Maxine; f; 6 (7-20-26); F; s; dau; yes; yes; A

GOOTKA

404; Enoch; m; 59 (1873); F; s; Head; yes; yes; C

GOYA

405; Lucas; m; 40 (1892); F; m; Head; yes; yes; G
406; Millie; f; 34 (1898); F; s; wife; yes; yes; G
407; Mildred; f; 16 (1916); F; s; dau; yes; yes; G
408; Robert; m; 9 (1923); F; s; son; yes; yes; G
409; Kenneth; m; 8 (1924); F; s; son; yes; yes; G
410; Julia; f; 6 (1926); F; s; dau; yes; yes; G
411; Leslie; m; 2 (1930); F; s; son; yes; yes; G

HAHHE

412; [Blank]; f; 45 (1887); F; w; Head; yes; yes; B

HALYVE

413; Saul; m; 41 (1891); F; m; Head; yes; yes; D
414; Josie; f; 38 (1894); F; m; wife; yes; yes; D
415; Mary Burdette; f; 19 (1913); F; s; dau; yes; yes; D
416; Ernest; m; 17 (1915); F; s; son; yes; yes; D

HOPI INDIAN CENSUS, (As of April 1, 1932)

KEY: Census Number; Name; Sex; Age at Last Birthday; Tribe (Hopi, unless otherwise stated); Degree of Blood; Marital Status; Relationship to Head of Family; At Jurisdiction where enrolled [Yes or No] (If no, Where); Ward [Yes or No]; Hopi Village [according to key].

HANAHYU

417; Saasie; m; 71 (1861); F; m; Head; yes; yes; B
418; Tubawcie; f; 64 (1868); F; m; wife; yes; yes; B

HARRIS

419; George; m; 38 (1895); F; m; Head; yes; yes; D
420; (Dawyonema), Dot; f; 31 (1901); F; m; wife; yes; yes; D
421; Everett; m; 16 (1916); F; s; son; yes; yes; D
422; Sylvia; f; 14 (1918); F; s; dau; yes; yes; D
423; Justin; m; 10 (1922); F; s; son; yes; yes; D
424; Darrie; m; 7 (1925); F; s; son; yes; yes; D
425; Alvin; m; 3 (1929); F; s; son; yes; yes; D
426; Eric; m; 1 (9-10-30); F; s; son; yes; yes; D

HARVEY

427; Clyde; m; 35 (1897); F; m; Head; yes; yes; C
428; Theresa; f; 27 (1905); F; m; wife; yes; yes; C
429; Ola; f; 7 (1925); F; s; dau; yes; yes; C
430; Gilman; m; 5 (9-1-26); F; s; son; yes; yes; C
431; Felix; m; 3 (11-3-28); F; s; son; yes; yes; C
432; Milton; m; 1 (3-21-31); F; s; son; yes; yes; C

HASKEE

433; David; m; 42 (1890); F; m; Head; yes; yes; G
434; Ada; f; 39 (1893); F; m; wife; yes; yes; G
435; Agnes; f; 17 (1915); F; s; dau; yes; yes; G
436; Helen; f; ?; F; s; dau; yes; yes; G
437; Katherine; f; 13 (1919); F; s; dau; yes; yes; G
438; Vona; f; ?; F; s; dau; yes; yes; G
439; Leona; f; 8 (1924); F; s; dau; yes; yes; G
440; Elveria; f; 6 (1926); F; s; dau; yes; yes; G

HAYAH

441; [Blank]; m; 71 (1861); F; w; Head; yes; yes; B

HEALING

442; Willie; m; 50 (1882); F; m; Head; yes; yes; A
443; Amie; f; 48 (1884); F; m; wife; yes; yes; A

17

KEY: Census Number; Name; Sex; Age at Last Birthday; Tribe (Hopi, unless otherwise stated); Degree of Blood; Marital Status; Relationship to Head of Family; At Jurisdiction where enrolled [Yes or No] (If no, Where); Ward [Yes or No]; Hopi Village [according to key].

444; Dewey; m; 25 (1907); F; s; son; yes; yes; A
445; Fletcher; m; 23 (1909); F; s; son; yes; yes; A
446; Lucia; f; 8 (1924); F; s; dau; yes; yes; A

HENNEQUAFTEWA

447; Andrew; m; 55 (1877); F; m; Head; yes; yes; F
448; Ella; f; 48 (1884); F; m; wife; yes; yes; F
449; Lee; m; 24 (1908); F; s; son; yes; yes; F
450; Sidney; m; 19 (1913); F; s; son; yes; yes; F
451; Alice; f; 24 (1908); F; s; dau; yes; yes; F

HERMEHOEWA

452; [Blank]; m; 66 (1866); F; m; Head; yes; yes; D
453; (Kashwiaema), [Blank]; f; 74 (1858); F; m; wife; yes; yes; D
454; **Cashoya**, Archie; m; 27 (1905); F; s; son; yes; yes; D
455; **Secahonka**, Mardell; f; 18 (1914); F; s; grd-dau; yes; yes; D
456; **Lomayestewa**, Renspie; m; 15 (1917); F; s; grd-son; yes; yes; D

HERMEHONGOVA

457; Charley; m; 53 (1879); F; m; Head; yes; yes; E
458; (Sewenka), [Blank]; f; 57 (1875); F; m; wife; yes; yes; E

HERMESTA

459; [Blank]; m; 59 (1873); F; w; Head; yes; yes; I

HERMEVEHEMA

460; Vance; m; 46 (1886); F; s; Head; yes; yes; E

HERMINGNEWA

461; Tom; m; 50 (1882); F; w; Head; yes; yes; D
462; **Coochinema**, Judith; f; 24 (1908); F; s; dau; yes; yes; D
463; **Quanuysie**, Olive; f; 20 (1912); F; s; dau; yes; yes; D

HOAHTEWA

464; [Blank]; m; 46 (1886); F; m; Head; yes; yes; I
465; (Talashongin), [Blank]; f; 51 (1881); F; m; wife; yes; yes; I
466; **Ahtutu**, Bruce; m; 27 (1905); F; s; stp-son; yes; yes; I

18

KEY: Census Number; Name; Sex; Age at Last Birthday; Tribe (Hopi, unless otherwise stated); Degree of Blood; Marital Status; Relationship to Head of Family; At Jurisdiction where enrolled [Yes or No] (If no, Where); Ward [Yes or No]; Hopi Village [according to key].

467; **Talachongin**, Harriet; f; 18 (1914); F; s; stp-dau; yes; yes; I
468; **Lemahwyma**, Grey; m; 16 (1916); F; s; grd-son; yes; yes; I

HOBBU

469; Harvey; m; 60 (1872); F; m; Head; yes; yes; A
470; Lucy; f; 54 (1878); F; m; wife; yes; yes; A

HOMANA

471; Herbert; m; 34 (1898); F; m; Head; yes; yes; G
472; Lily; f; 35 (1897); F; m; wife; yes; yes; G
473; Florine; f; 12 (1920); F; s; dau; yes; yes; G
474; Dorothy; f; 10 (1922); F; s; dau; yes; yes; G
475; Virginia; f; 5 (4-13-26); F; s; dau; yes; yes; G
476; Tracy; m; 3 (9-22-28); F; s; son; yes; yes; G
477; Walter; m; 1 (10-23-30); F; s; son; yes; yes; G

HOMEWYTEWA

478; Homer; m; 41 (1891); F; m; Head; yes; yes; G
479; Eva; f; 37 (1895); F; m; wife; yes; yes; G
480; Dorothy; f; 16 (1916); F; s; dau; yes; yes; G
481; Isabel; f; 12 (1920); F; s; dau; yes; yes; G
482; Roosevelt; m; 10 (1922); F; s; son; yes; yes; G
483; Byron; m; 7 (1925); F; s; son; yes; yes; G
484; Martha; f; 5 (2-22-27); F s; dau; yes; yes; G
485; Delphina; f; 2 (4-5-29); F; s; dau; yes; yes; G
486; Adeline; f; 1 (2-15-31); F; s; dau; yes; yes; G

HOMIKNI

487; [Blank]; m; 94 (1838); F; w; Head; yes; yes; G
488; [Blank]; m; 62 (1870); F; s; son; yes; yes; G

HONANI

489; George; m; 42 (1890); F; m; Head; yes; yes; G
490; Esther; f; 40 (1892); F; m; wife; yes; yes; G
491; Clarence; m; 20 (1912); F; s; son; yes; yes; G
492; Jimmy; m; 17 (1915); F; s; son; yes; yes; G
493; Neva; f; 15 (1917); F; s; dau; yes; yes; G
494; Dorothy; f; 14 (1918); F; s; dau; yes; yes; G
495; Gilbert; m; 11 (1921); F; s; son; yes; yes; G

KEY: Census Number; Name; Sex; Age at Last Birthday; Tribe (Hopi, unless otherwise stated); Degree of Blood; Marital Status; Relationship to Head of Family; At Jurisdiction where enrolled [Yes or No] (If no, Where); Ward [Yes or No]; Hopi Village [according to key].

496; Jackson; m; 3 (1929); F; s; son; yes; yes; G
497; Alice; f; 1 (1-6-31); F; s; dau; yes; yes; G

498; Judge; m; 82 (1850); F; m; Head; yes; yes; F
499; [Blank]; f; 82 (1850); F; m; wife; yes; yes; F

500; Steve; m; 30 (1902); F; m; Head; yes; yes; F
501; Elsie; f; 29 (1903); F; m; wife; yes; yes; F

502; Thomas; m; 54 (1878); F; m; Head; yes; yes; F
503; Daisy; f; 30 (1893); F; m; wife; yes; yes; G
504; Marian; f; 17 (1915); F; s; dau; yes; yes; F
505; Alberta; f; 16 (1916); F; s; dau; yes; yes; F
506; George; m; 15 (1917); m; s; son; yes; yes; F
507; Ethel; f; 14 (1918); F; s; son; yes; yes; F
508; Evaline; f; 12 (1920); F; s; dau; yes; yes; F
509; Emory; m; 7 (1925); F; s; son; yes; yes; F
510; Noble; m; 3 (4-29-28); F; s; son; yes; yes; F

HONE

511; [Blank]; m; 71 (1861);F; m; Head; yes; yes; A
512; Quanka; f; 64 (1868); F; m; wife; yes; yes; A
513; **Crome**, Sarah; f; 29 (1903); F; m; dau; no; P.O. Santa Anita, Los Angeles Co, CA; yes; [village not given]
514; Otto; m; 26 (1906); F; s; son; yes; yes; A
515; Arthur; m; 23 (1909); F; s; son; yes; yes; A
516; Celia; f; 18 (1914); F; s; dau; yes; yes; A
517; **Crome**, Harry Walter; m; 5 (1927); ½; s; grd-son; no; P.O. Santa Anita, Los Angeles Co, CA; yes; [village not given]

HONWAHTEWA

518; Calvin; m; 62 (1870); F; m; Head; yes; yes; F
519; Cynthia; f; 61 (1871); F; m; wife; yes; yes; F
520; Donald; m; 15 (1917); F; s; son; yes; yes; F
521; **Poshoktooma**, Preston; m; 14 (1918); F; s; grnd-son; yes; yes; F
522; **Poshoktooma**, David; m; 8 (1924); F; s; grnd-son; yes; yes; F

HONEWAHTEWA

523; Louis; m; 21 (1911); F; m; Head; yes; yes; F
524; Edith; f; 20 (1912); F; m; wife; yes; yes; F
525; Louis Calvin; m; 1 (?-30-30); F; s; son; yes; yes; F

20

HOPI INDIAN CENSUS, (As of April 1, 1932)

KEY: Census Number; Name; Sex; Age at Last Birthday; Tribe (Hopi, unless otherwise stated); Degree of Blood; Marital Status; Relationship to Head of Family; At Jurisdiction where enrolled [Yes or No] (If no, Where); Ward [Yes or No]; Hopi Village [according to key].

HONGEVA

526; Hooker; m; 76 (1856)l F; m; Head; yes; yes; B
527; Sophepmene; f; 67 (1865); F; m; wife; yes; yes; B

HONHANGAVA

528; Ralph Chas; m; 27 (1905); F; m; Head; yes; yes; F
529; Sybil; f; 28 (1906); F; m; wife; yes; yes; F
530; James Oren; m; 9/12 (6-16-31); F; s; son; yes; yes; F

HONUMPTIE

531; Leslie; m; 29 (1903); F; m; Head; yes; yes; F
532; Betty; f; 26 (1906); F; m; wife; yes; yes; F
533; Arle; m; 8 (1926); F; s; son; yes; yes; F
534; Calvin; m; 4 (1928); F; s; son; yes; yes; F

HOOMANIFKA

535; Clyde; m; 37 (1895); F; m; Head; yes; yes; F
536; Nora; f; 32 (1900); F; m; wife; yes; yes; F

HORZASQUAPUH

537; [Blank]; f; 88 (1844); F; w; Head; yes; yes; E
538; **Masihonsie**, Inez; f; 27 (1905); F; s; grnd- dau; yes; yes; E

HOWATO

539; Edward; m; 39 (1893); F; m; Head; yes; yes; B
540; Viola; f; 35 (1897); F; m; wife; yes; yes; B
541; Walter Howard; m; 11 (1921); F; s; son; yes; yes; B
542; Clara Flint; f; 7 (1925); F; s; dau; yes; yes; B
543; Nina; f; 4 (2-8-28); V; s; dau; yes; yes; B
544; Lester; m; 1/12 (3-18-32); F; s; son; yes; yes; B

HOYISVA

545; Pierce; m; 42 (1890); F; s; Head; yes; yes; G

HOYEWESVA

546; Amos; m; 29 (1903); F; m; Head; yes; yes; I

21

HOPI INDIAN CENSUS, (As of April 1, 1932)

KEY: Census Number; Name; Sex; Age at Last Birthday; Tribe (Hopi, unless otherwise stated); Degree of Blood; Marital Status; Relationship to Head of Family; At Jurisdiction where enrolled [Yes or No] (If no, Where); Ward [Yes or No]; Hopi Village [according to key].

547; Theresa; f; 28 (1904); F; m; wife; yes; yes; I
548; Stella Flora; f; 3 (1929); F; s; dau; yes; yes; I
549; Roy; m; 3/12 (9-6-31); F; s; son; yes; yes; I

HOYUNGA

550; Silas; m; 29 (1903); F; m; Head; yes; yes; I
551; Priscilla; f; 27 (1905); F; m; wife; yes; yes; I
552; Robert; m; 1 (4-19-30); F; s; son; yes; yes; I
553; Silas, Jr; m; 9/12 (6-30-31); F; s; son; yes; yes; I
554; **Talaseumka**, [Blank]; f; 54 (1878); F; w; mother-in-law; yes; yes; I
555; **Sekahonsie**, Jane; f; 21 (1911); F; s; sis-in-law; yes; yes; I
556; **Sakaquesva**, Jasper; m; 18 (1914); F; s; bro-in-law; yes; yes; I
557; [Blank], Nelson; m; 12 (1920); F; s; bro-in-law; yes; yes; I

HUMA

558; Story; m; 33 (1899); F; m; Head; yes; yes; B
559; Violet; f; 32 (1900); F; m; wife; yes; yes; B
560; Story, Jr; m; 10 (1922); F; s; son; yes; yes; B
561; David; m; 8 (1924); F; s; son; yes; yes; B
562; Anita; f; 5 (10-7-28); F; s; dau; yes; yes; B
563; Wilson; m; 11/12 (4-24-31); F; s; son; yes; yes; B
564; Celeste; f; 20 (1912); F; s; sister; yes; yes; B
565; Val Jean; m; 17 (1915); F; s; bro; yes; yes; B

HUMAIKWAIMA

566; Grover; m; 68 (1864); F; m; Head; yes; yes; G
567; Dora; f; 67 (1865); F; m; wife; yes; yes; G
568; Allen; m; 25 (1907); F; s; son; yes; yes; G

HUMOUMPTEWA

569; Smiley; m; 68 (1864); F; m; Head; yes; yes; D
570; Selma; f; 52 (1880); F; m; wife; yes; yes; D
571; **Secakuku**, Joseph; m; 35 (1897); F; m; son; yes; yes; D
572; **Talah**, Jale; m; 25 (1907); F; s; son; yes; yes; D

HUMILETSTIWA

573; Luke; m; 30 (1902); F; m; Head; yes; yes; G
574; Mabel; f; 28 (1904); F; m; wife; yes; yes; G

22

KEY: Census Number; Name; Sex; Age at Last Birthday; Tribe (Hopi, unless otherwise stated); Degree of Blood; Marital Status; Relationship to Head of Family; At Jurisdiction where enrolled [Yes or No] (If no, Where); Ward [Yes or No]; Hopi Village [according to key].

HUMPHREY

575; Tom; m; ?; F; m; Head; yes; yes; I
576; Marietta; f; 25 (1907); F; m; wife; yes; yes; I

HUMYESVA

577; Joshua; m; 65 (1867); F; w; Head; yes; yes; F
578; Mervin; m; 26 (1906); F; s; son; yes; yes; F

HOVALE

579; Luke; m; 26 (1906); F; m; Head; yes; yes; B
580; (Hunter), Irma; f; 35 (1897); F; m; wife; yes; yes; B
581; [**Hunter**], Allen; m; 18 (1914); F; s; yes; yes; B
582; [**Hunter**], Janey; f; 17 (1915); F; s; dau yes; yes; B
583; [**Hunter**], Roland; m; 13 (1919); F; s; son; yes; yes; B
584; [**Hunter**], Dart; m; 10 (1922); F; s; son; yes; yes; B
585; [**Hunter**], Edgar M; m; 8 (1924); F; s; son; yes; yes; B
586; Zora; f; 2/12 (1-30-32); F; s; dau; yes; yes; B
587; **Hunocke**, [Blank]; f; 70 (1862); F; w; mother-in-law; yes; yes; B

HYEOMA

588; Hastings; m; 36 (1896); F; m; Head; yes; yes; E
589; (Talashoenema), Edna; f; 28 (1904); F; m; wife; yes; yes; E
590; Lucius; m; 22 (1921); F; s; son; yes; yes; E
591; Calvin; m; 9 (1923); F; s; son; yes; yes; E
592; Elva; f; (1925); F; s; dau; yes; yes; E
593; Bernie Lee; m; 4 (10-6-27); F; s; son; yes; yes; E
594; Lydia; f; 2 (11025029); F; s; dau; yes; yes; E

JAMES

595; Claude; m; 40 (1892); F; m; Head; yes; yes; G
596; Alice; f; 34 (1898); F; m; wife; yes; yes; G
597; Etta; f; 17 (1915); F; s; dau; yes; yes; G
598; Elda; f; 16 (1916); F; s; dau; yes; yes; G
599; Rita; f; 11 (1921); F; s; dau; yes; yes; G
600; Bessie; f; 4 (8-8-27); F; s; dau; yes; yes; G
601; Elizabeth; f; 2 (4-12-28); F; s; dau; yes; yes; G
602; Linden; m; 1/12 (2-21-32); F; s; son; yes; yes; G

HOPI INDIAN CENSUS, (As of April 1, 1932)

KEY: Census Number; Name; Sex; Age at Last Birthday; Tribe (Hopi, unless otherwise stated); Degree of Blood; Marital Status; Relationship to Head of Family; At Jurisdiction where enrolled [Yes or No] (If no, Where); Ward [Yes or No]; Hopi Village [according to key].

603; Quincy; m; 37 (1895); F; m; Head; yes; yes; G
604; Nannie; f; 34 (1898); F; m; wife; yes; yes; G

[**NOTE**: #605 was omitted on original list.]

606; Seba; m; 45 (1887); F; m; Head; yes; yes; G
607; Effie; f; 41 (1891); ½; m; wife; yes; yes; G
608; Rose Lee; f; 19 (1913); F; s; dau; yes; yes; G
609; Elsie; f; 17 (1915); F; s; dau; yes; yes; G
610; Mayfair; f; 13 (1919); F; s; dau; yes; yes; G
611; Dalton; m; 9 (1923); F; s; son; yes; yes; G
612; Leona; f; 7 (1925); F; s; dau; yes; yes; G
613; Emmett; m; 4 (4-7-27); F; s; son; yes; yes; G
614; Jean; f; 2; (1930); F; s; dau; yes; yes; G
615; Caroline; f; 1 (7-7-30); F; s; dau; yes; yes; G

JENKINS

616; Sam; m; 46 (1887); F; m; Head; yes; yes; G
617; Lavina; f; 35 (1897); F; m; wife; yes; yes; G
618; Janet; f; 15 (1917); F; s; dau; yes; yes; G
619 Marshall; m; 14 (1918); F; s; son; yes; yes; G
620; Ethel; f; 23; (1920); F; s; dau; yes; yes; G
621; Fomona; f; 11 (1921); F; s; dau; yes; yes; G
622; Lucinda; f; 9 (1923); F; s; dau; yes; yes; G
623; Palmer; m; 7 (1925); F; s; son; yes; yes; G
624; Violet; f; 4 (10-15-27); F; s; dau; yes; yes; G
625; Peter; m; 2 (2-2-30); F; s; son; yes; yes; G

626; Tom; m; 47 (1885); F; m; Head; yes; yes; G
627; Anna; f; 41 (1891); F; m; wife; yes; yes; G
628; Samuel; m; 21 (1911); F; s; son; yes; yes; G
629; Calvin; m; 12 (1920); F; s; son; yes; yes; G
630; Clara Belle; f; 9 (1923); F; s; dau; yes; yes; G

JOHNSON

631; Fred; m; 29 (1903); F; m; Head; yes; yes; G
632; Minnie; f; 36 (1896); F; m; wife; yes; yes; G
633; Rachael; f; 9 (1923); F; s; dau; yes; yes; G
634; Alice; f; 7 (1925); F; s; dau; yes; yes; G
635; Edith; f; 4 (3-4-27); F; s; dau; yes; yes; G
636; Vina; f; 1 (11-1-29); F; s; dau; yes; yes; G

24

HOPI INDIAN CENSUS, (As of April 1, 1932)

KEY: Census Number; Name; Sex; Age at Last Birthday; Tribe (Hopi, unless otherwise stated); Degree of Blood; Marital Status; Relationship to Head of Family; At Jurisdiction where enrolled [Yes or No] (If no, Where); Ward [Yes or No]; Hopi Village [according to key].

637; Tillie; f; 35 (1897); F; s; Head; yes; yes; G
638; Wilhemena; f; 3 (8-21-28); F; s; dau; yes; yes; G

639; Tuvaletstiwa; m; 55 (1877); F; w; Head; yes; yes; G
640; Frisco; m; 26 (1906); F; s; son; yes; yes; G
641; Helen; f; 16 (1916); F; s; dau; yes; yes; G

JOHNNY

642; Lily; f; 41 (1891); F; w; Head; yes; yes; G
643; Arlene; f; 14 (1918); F; s; dau; yes; yes; G
644; Donald; m; 12 (1920); F; s; son; yes; yes; G

JOHONET

645; Paul; m; 23 (1909); F; m; Head; yes; yes; I
646; (Sehongva), Janet; f; 20 (1912); F; m; wife; yes; yes; I

JOSEWYTEWA

647; Glenn; m; 57 (1875); F; m; Head; yes; yes; F
648; Clara; f; 37 (1895); F; m; wife; yes; yes; F
649; Marjorie; f; 20 (1912); F; s; dau; yes; yes; F
650; Rose; f; 12 (1920); F; s; dau; yes; yes; F
651; Ray; m; 10 (1922); F; s; son; yes; yes; F
652; Cyrus; m; 4 (1928); F; s; son; yes; yes; F
653; Jackson; m; 8/12 (6-2-31); F; s; son; yes; yes; F

JOSHONGAVA

654; Major; m; 61 (1871); F; m; Head; yes; yes; F
655; Madeline; f; 61 (1871); F; m; wife; yes; yes; F
656; Walter; m; 22 (1910); F; s; son; yes; yes; F
657; Alfred; m; 16 (1916); F; s; son; yes; yes; F

KAHBOOTEMA

658; John; m; 60 (1872); F; m; Head; yes; yes; B
659; Maggie; f; 44 (1888); F; m; wife; yes; yes; B
660; Phyllis; f; 27 (1905); F; s; dau; yes; yes; B
661; Alex Womack; m; 10 (1913); F; s; son; yes; yes; B
662; Alfred; m; 11 (1921); F; s; son; yes; yes; B

HOPI INDIAN CENSUS, (As of April 1, 1932)

KEY: Census Number; Name; Sex; Age at Last Birthday; Tribe (Hopi, unless otherwise stated); Degree of Blood; Marital Status; Relationship to Head of Family; At Jurisdiction where enrolled [Yes or No] (If no, Where); Ward [Yes or No]; Hopi Village [according to key].

KAISIE

663; Victor; m; 31 (1901); F; w; Head; yes; yes; B
664; Fred; m; 11 (1921); F; s; son; yes; yes; B

KALNOMTIWA

665; [Blank]; m; 58 (1874); F; m; Head; yes; yes; G
666; Nancy; f; 58 (1874); F; m; wife; yes; yes; G
667; Carl; m; 26 (1906); F; s; son; yes; yes; G

668; Julius; m; 28 (1904; F; m; Head; yes; yes; G
669; Emily; f; 24 (1908); F; m; wife; yes; yes; G
670; David; m; 1 (11-9-30); F; s; son; yes; yes; G

KARZOH

671; Flossie; f; 29 (1903); F; s; Head; yes; yes; E
672; Oren; m; 4 (1928); F; s; son; yes; yes; E
673; Leila Lee; f; 1 (12-4-30); f; s; dau; yes; yes; E

KASCHNIMENA

674; Sammy; m; 56 (1876); F; m; Head; yes; yes; F
675; Pauline; f; 57 (1875); F; m; wife; yes; yes; F
676; **Joseumptewa**, [Blank]; m; 69 (1863); F; w; father-in-law; yes; yes; F
677; **Nevawutewa**, Amos; m; 64 (1868); F; w; bro-in-law; yes; yes; F
678; **Pumahooya**, Geneva; f; 16 (1916); F; s; niece; yes; yes; F
679; **Pumahooya**, Myrtle; f; 12 (1920); F; s; niece; yes; yes; F

KAVONA

680; Frank; m; 35 (1897); F; m; Head; yes; yes; C
681; Rona; f; 33 (1899); F; m; wife; yes; yes; C
682; Bessie; f; 9 (1923); F; s; dau; yes; yes; C
683; Wilbur; m; 4 (1928); F; s; son; yes; yes; C

KEWAHNE

684; [Blank]; m; 56 (1876); F; w; Head; yes; yes; A
685; Lincoln; m; 32 (1900); F; s; son; yes; yes; A

26

HOPI INDIAN CENSUS, (As of April 1, 1932)

KEY: Census Number; Name; Sex; Age at Last Birthday; Tribe (Hopi, unless otherwise stated); Degree of Blood; Marital Status; Relationship to Head of Family; At Jurisdiction where enrolled [Yes or No] (If no, Where); Ward [Yes or No]; Hopi Village [according to key].

KEWANEOSEE

686; Luke; m; 60 (1872); F; m; Head; yes; yes; D
687; (Tewanginema), Vivian; f; 44 (1888); F; m; wife; yes; yes; D
688; Dwight; m; 13 (1919); F; s; son; yes; yes; D
689; Charles; m; 9 (1924); F; s; son; yes; yes; D

KEWANHONGVA

690; Lodge; m; 55 (1877); F; m; Head; yes; yes; E
691; (Yoyowynema), [Blank]; f; 64 (1868); F; m; wife; yes; yes; E
692; **Talasvensie**, Lucille; f; 19 (1914); F; s; dau; yes; yes; E

KEWANIMPTEVA

693; [Blank]; m; ?; F; w; Head; yes; yes; F

KEWANIMPTEWA

694; [Blank]; m; 55 (1877); F; m; Head; yes; yes; H
695; Quemanenim; f; 53 (1879); F; m; wife; yes; yes; H
696; Harry; m; 26 (1906); F; s; son; yes; yes; H
697; Davis; m; 12 (1920); F; s; son; yes; yes; H

KEWANQUAPNIM

698; [Blank]; m; 93 (1839); F; w; Head; yes; yes; H

KEWANSEOMA

699; [Blank]; m; 75 (1858); F; w; Head; yes; yes; D
700; **Shupula**, [Blank]; m; 15 (1917); F; s; grnd-son; yes; yes; D

KEWANVAYMA

701; Lincoln; m; 57 (1875); F; m; Head; yes; yes; F
702; Hannah; f; 57 (1875); F; m; wife; yes; yes; F
703; **Koochymptewa**, [Blank]; m; 62 (1870); F; w; bro-in-law; yes; yes; F
704; **Ditzkie**, Alexander; m; 22 (1910); F; s; nephew; yes; yes; F

KEWANVEMA

705; Matthew; m; 44 (1888); F; m; Head; yes; yes; F
706; Clara Kate; f; 41 (1891); F; m; wife; yes; yes; F

HOPI INDIAN CENSUS, (As of April 1, 1932)

KEY: Census Number; Name; Sex; Age at Last Birthday; Tribe (Hopi, unless otherwise stated); Degree of Blood; Marital Status; Relationship to Head of Family; At Jurisdiction where enrolled [Yes or No] (If no, Where); Ward [Yes or No]; Hopi Village [according to key].

707; Lloyd; m; 19 (1913); F; s; son; yes; yes; F
708; Clarence; m; 12 (1920); F; s; son; yes; yes; F
709; Eugene; m; 10 (1922); F; s; son; yes; yes; F
710; Lucian; m; 5 (9-12-26); F; s; son; yes; yes; F

711; William; m; 56 (1876); F; w; Head; yes; yes; F
712; Janet; f; 23 (1909); F; s; dau; yes; yes; F
713; Ellen; f; 20 (1912); F; s; dau; yes; yes; F
714; Tirzah; f; 16 (1916); F; s; dau; yes; yes; F
715; Hubert; m; 14; (1918); F; s; son; yes; yes; F
716; Ernest; m; 12 (1920); F; s; son; yes; yes; F
717; Kathleen; f; 11 (1921); F; s; dau; yes; yes; F
718; Adell; f; 6 (1926); F; s; dau; yes; yes; F

KEWANVEYEWMA or KEWANVEYWMA

719; Marshall; m; 47 (1885); F; m; Head; yes; yes; F
720; Zola; f; 40 (1892); F; m; wife; yes; yes; F
721; Ida; f; 13 (1919); F; s; dau; yes; yes; F
722; Jane; f; 12 (1920); F; s; dau; yes; yes; F
723; Harmon; m; 7 (1925); F; s; son; yes; yes; F
724; Gilbert H; m; 3 (4-1-29); F; s; son; yes; yes; F

[NOTE: The above last name was spelled both ways.]

KEWANWYTEWA

725; Jim; m; 37 (1896); F; w; Head; yes; yes; G
726; Flora; f; 9 (1923); F; s; dau; yes; yes; G
727; Willis; m; 8 (1924); F; s; son; yes; yes; G
728; Oren Davis; m; 6 (8-17-26); F; s; son; yes; yes; G
729; Warren; m; 11/12 (4-25-31); F; s; son; yes; yes; G

KOCHHONOWAH

730; David; m; 61 (1871); F; m; Head; yea; yes; C
731; Tema; f; 46 (1886); f; m; wife; yes; yes; C
732; Irma; f; 26 (1906); F; s; dau; yes; yes; C
733; Randolph; m; 20 (1912); F; s; son; yes; yes; C
734; Mildred; f; 17 (1915); F; s; dau; yes; yes; C
735; Elliott; m; 12 (1920); F; s; son; yes; yes; C

HOPI INDIAN CENSUS, (As of April 1, 1932)

KEY: Census Number; Name; Sex; Age at Last Birthday; Tribe (Hopi, unless otherwise stated); Degree of Blood; Marital Status; Relationship to Head of Family; At Jurisdiction where enrolled [Yes or No] (If no, Where); Ward [Yes or No]; Hopi Village [according to key].

KOMAHWOCKTA

736; [Blank]; m; 92 (1841); F; w; Head; yes; yes; I

KOMALAUTEWA

737; [Blank]; m; 63 (1869); F; m; Head; yes; yes; D
738; (Cashyownoma), Daisy; f; 53 (1879); F; m; wife; yes; yes; D
739; **Josumpke**, Hollis; f; 26 (1906); F; s; dau; yes; yes; D
740; **Josvenka**, Mildred; f; 18 (1914); F; s; dau; yes; yes; D
741; **Bakyoya**, Carol; f; 5 (12-25-26); F; s; grnd-dau; yes; yes; D
742; **Kayama**, Elizabeth; f; 3 (5-18-28); F; s; grnd-dau; yes; yes; D

KOMANIMPTEWA

743; [Blank]; m; 60 (1872); F; m; Head; yes; yes; D
744; (Kowanaynoma), [Blank]; f; 62 (1870); F; m; wife; yes; yes; D
745; **Sequama**, Lloyd; m; 26 (1906); F; s; son; yes; yes; D
746; **Honheftewa**, Atch; m; 23 (1909); F; s; son; yes; yes; D
747; **Atokuku**, Don; m; 41 (1891); F; s; stp-son; yes; yes; D
748; **Chamema**, Mark; m; 36 (1896); F; s; stp-son; yes; yes; D
749; **Tawanuzsu**, Conrad; m; 27 (1905); F; s; stp-son; yes; yes; D
750; **Talaswensie**, Loeta; f; 18 (1914); F; s; grnd-dau; yes; yes; D

KOMOLETSTEWA

751; Austin; m; 16 (1916); F; s; Head; yes; yes; D

KOMYESTEWA

752; [Blank]; f; 62 (1870); F; w; Head; yes; yes; F

KOMYUCIE

753; [Blank]; f; 57 (1875); F; w; Head; yes; yes; B

KOMYYAVA

754; [Blank]; m; 58 (1874); F; m; Head; yes; yes; F
755; Callie; f; 57 (1875); F; m; wife; yes; yes; F
756; Marie; f; 19 (1913); F; s; dau; yes; yes; F

KEY: Census Number; Name; Sex; Age at Last Birthday; Tribe (Hopi, unless otherwise stated); Degree of Blood; Marital Status; Relationship to Head of Family; At Jurisdiction where enrolled [Yes or No] (If no, Where); Ward [Yes or No]; Hopi Village [according to key].

KONYVMA

757; Spencer; m; 27 (1905); F; m; Head; yes; yes; F
758; Florence; f; 23 (1909); F; m; wife; yes; yes; F
759; Herbert; m; 3 (1929); F; s; son; yes; yes; F
760: Roberta; f; 6/12 (11-26-31); F; s; dau; yes; yes; F

KOOCHEOMA

761; [Blank]; m; 66 (1866); F; m; Head; yes; yes; I
762; Mayesnim; f; 64 (1868); F; m; wife; yes; yes; I
763; Franklin; m; 23 (1909); F; s; son; yes; yes; I

KOOCHONGOVA

764; Dan; m; 51 (1881); F; m; Head; yes; yes; I
765; (Nuvyesnim), Neah; f; 44 (1888); F; m; wife; yes; yes; I
766; Jackson; m; 20 (1912); F; s; stp-son; yes; yes; I
767; Lucille; f; 18 (1914); F; s; stp-dau; yes; yes; I
768; Rhoda; f; 13 (1919); F; s; stp-dau; yes; yes; I

KOOSYUMKA

769; [Blank]; f; 62 (1870); F; w; Head; yes; yes; I
770; **Wishibbe**, Edward; m; 35 (1897); F; w; son; yes; yes; I
771; **Wishibbe**, Edna; f; 10 (1922); F; s; grnd-dau; yes; yes; I

KOOTSHOENEWA

772; Jack; m; 42 (1890); F; m; Head; yes; yes; I
773; Sarah; f; 34 (1898); F; m; wife; yes; yes; I
774; Neil; m; 17 (1915); F; s; son; yes; yes; I
775; **Pahuhunim**, Jennie; f; 11 (1921); F; s; stp-dau; yes; yes; I

KOOTSHONGSIE

776; [Blank]; f; 51(1881); F; w; Head; yes; yes; I
777; Eva; f; 21 (1911); F; s; dau; yes; yes; I
778; James; m; 15 (1917); F; s; son; yes; yes; I
779; Leslie; m; 12 (1920); F; s; son; yes; yes; I

KOOTSHOYOOMA

780; Wallace; m; 49 (1883); F; m; Head; yes; yes; I

KEY: Census Number; Name; Sex; Age at Last Birthday; Tribe (Hopi, unless otherwise stated); Degree of Blood; Marital Status; Relationship to Head of Family; At Jurisdiction where enrolled [Yes or No] (If no, Where); Ward [Yes or No]; Hopi Village [according to key].

781; **Pahuminka**, [Blank]; f; 57 (1875); F; m; wife; yes; yes; I
782; **Pahuse**, Gordon; m; 20 (1912); F; s; nephew; yes; yes; I
783; **Pahuse**, Fred; m; 19 (1913); F; s; nephew; yes; yes; I
784; **Pahuse**, Alida; f; 16 (1916); F; s; niece; yes; yes; I

KOOTSNOEVA

785; [Blank]; m; 63 (1869); F; m; Head; yes; yes; I
786; (Navahongnim), [Blank]; f; 54 (1878); F; m; wife; yes; yes; I

KOOTSVOYEOMA

787; [Blank]; m; 69 (1863); F; m; yes; yes; I
788; Honanoya; f; 64 (1868); F; m; wife; yes; yes; I
*787; Jean; f; 20 (1912); F; s; dau; yes; yes; I
*788; Lorene; f; 16 (1916); F; s; dau; yes; yes; I
789; **Temoseoma**, Newton; m; 10 (1922); F; s; son; yes; yes; I
790; **Tewanimptewa**, Edward; m; 49 (1883); F; s; bro-in-law; yes; yes; I

[***NOTE:** Numbered according to original]

KOOTSVAYEOMA

791; Lamuel; m; 25 (1907); F; m; Head; yes; yes; I
792; Daisy; f; 31 (1901); F; m; wife; yes; yes; I
793; Monroe; m; 2 (10-31-20); F; s; son; yes; yes; I
794; **Quapnimptewa**, Arnold; m; 9 (1923); F; s; stp-son; yes; yes; I
795; **Lomahwyma**, Gladys; f; 5 (1927); F; s; stp-dau; yes; yes; I
796; Connie; f; 6/12 (9-30-31); F; s; dau; yes; yes; I

KOOTSWATEWA

797; Theodore; m; 41 (1891); F; m; Head; yes; yes; I
798; Daisy; f; 39 (1893); F; m; wife; yes; yes; I
799; Marion; f; 18 (1914); F; s; dau; yes; yes; I
800; Byron; m; 16 (1916); F; s; son; yes; yes; I
801; Kate; f; 14 (1918); F; s; dau; yes; yes; I
802; Wade; m; 11 (1921); F; s; son; yes; yes; I
803; Arline; f; 7 (1925); F; s; dau; yes; yes; I
804; Ansel; m; 3 (1929); F; s; son; yes; yes; I

KOOYAQUAPTEWA

805; Ray; m; 41 (1891); F; m; Head; yes; yes; A

HOPI INDIAN CENSUS, (As of April 1, 1932)

KEY: Census Number; Name; Sex; Age at Last Birthday; Tribe (Hopi, unless otherwise stated); Degree of Blood; Marital Status; Relationship to Head of Family; At Jurisdiction where enrolled [Yes or No] (If no, Where); Ward [Yes or No]; Hopi Village [according to key].

806; Flora; f; 40 (1892); F; m; wife; yes; yes; A
807; Elliott S; m; 14 (1918); F; s; son; yes; yes; A
808; Warren; m; 12 (1920); F; s; son; yes; yes; A
809; Bertha; f; 9 (1923); F; s; dau; yes; yes; A
810; Harrison Ray; m; 7 (1925); F; s; son; yes; yes; A

KORUH

811; Simpson; m; 37 (1985); F; w; Head; yes; yes; F
812; Amelia; f; 11 (1921); F; s; dau; yes; yes; F
813; Harold; m; 8 (1924); F; s; son; yes; yes; F
814; Bell; f; 3 (1929); F; s; dau; yes; yes; F

KOYAHOEOMA

815; Joseph; m; 50 (1882); F; m; Head; yes; yes; F
816; Carrie; f; 47 (1885); F; m; wife; yes; yes; F
817; Agnes; f; 23 (1909); F; s; dau; yes; yes; F
818; Ernest; m; 18 (1914); F; s; son; yes; yes; F
819; Martha; f; 14 (1918); F; s; dau; yes; yes; F
820; Harold; m; 12 (1920); F; s; son; yes; yes; F
821; Jeffre; m; 10 (1922); F; s; son; yes; yes; F
822; August; m; 5 (8-3-26); F; s; son; yes; yes; F

KOYAHONEWA

823; [Blank]; m; 70(1862); F; m; Head; yes; yes; I
824; (Talahapnom), [Blank]; f; 67 (1865); F; m; wife; yes; yes; I
825; **Sewebence**, Lillie; f; 11 (1921); F; s; niece; yes; yes; I
826; **Kootsletstewa**, [Blank]; m; 45 (1887); F; s; bro-in-law; yes; yes; I

KOYAHONGOVA

827; [Blank]; m; 72 (1860); F; m; Head; yes; yes; I
828; Sonwysie; f; 70 (1862); F; m; wife; yes; yes; I
829; Herbert; m; 29 (1903); F; s; son; yes; yes; I
830; **Nasangoenim**, Ursula; f; 28 (1905); F; s; grnd-dau; yes; yes; I
831; **Talaswintewa**, Saul; m; 21 (1911); F; s; grnd-son; yes; yes; I
832; **Sakahongova**, Agnes; f; 11 (1921); F; s; grnd-dau; yes; yes; I
833; **Nasingoonim**, Leon; m; 3 (4-8-28); F; s; grnd-son; yes; yes; I

KOYAVENKA

834; Nettie; f; 44 (1888); F; s; Head; yes; yes; I

32

KEY: Census Number; Name; Sex; Age at Last Birthday; Tribe (Hopi, unless otherwise stated); Degree of Blood; Marital Status; Relationship to Head of Family; At Jurisdiction where enrolled [Yes or No] (If no, Where); Ward [Yes or No]; Hopi Village [according to key].

835; **Seethoema**, Kellar; m; 38 (1894); F; s; bro; yes; yes; I

KOYAWYTEWA

836; [Blank]; m; 72 (1860); F; m; Head; yes; yes; D
837; (Maswysic), [Blank]; f; 70 (1862); F; m; wife; yes; yes; D

KOYCHICE

838; Lois; f; 20 (1912); F; s; Head; yes; yes; I
839; Roy; m; 14 (1914); F; s; bro; yes; yes; I
840; Minnie; f; 12 (1920); F; s; sis; yes; yes; I

KOYOYUMPTEWA

841; [Blank]; m; 51 (1881); F; m; Head; yes; yes; I
842; Talahonsie; f; 48 1884); F; m; wife; yes; yes; I
843; Tillie; f; 20 (1912); F; s; dau; yes; yes; I
844; Homer; m; 16 (1916); F; s; son; yes; yes; I
845; Amelia; f; 10 (1922); F; s; dau; yes; yes; I

KUWANLEHTSIWMA

846; Laura; f; 52 (1880); F; w; Head; yes; yes; G
847; Lula; f; 19 (1913); F; s; dau; yes; yes; G
848; Louise; f; 16 (1916); F; s; dau; yes; yes; G
849; Martin; m; 13 (1919); F; s; son; yes; yes; G

KUWANVENIWMA

850; [Blank]; m; 78 (1854); F; w; Head; yes; yes; G

KUWANVENTIWA

851; [Blank]; m; 59 (1873); F; m; Head; yes; yes; G
852; Kate; f; 60 (1872); F; m; wife; yes; yes; G
853; Juanita; f; 21 (1911); F; s; dau; yes; yes; G
854; Hazel; f; 19 (1913); F; s; dau; yes; yes; G
855; Mike; m; 27 (1905); F; s; stp-son; yes; yes; G
856; Elsie; f; 23 (1909); F; s; stp-dau; yes; yes; G

KUWANWAYTIWA

857; [Blank]; m; 83 (1849); F; m; Head; yes; yes; G

KEY: Census Number; Name; Sex; Age at Last Birthday; Tribe (Hopi, unless otherwise stated); Degree of Blood; Marital Status; Relationship to Head of Family; At Jurisdiction where enrolled [Yes or No] (If no, Where); Ward [Yes or No]; Hopi Village [according to key].

858; Sakwapu; f; 61 (1871); F; m; wife; yes; yes; G

KUYANEMPTEWA

859; Robert; m; 50 (1882); F; w; Head; yes; yes; D
860; **Cyasurzah**, Ronald; m; 26 (1906); F; s; son; yes; yes; D
861; **Cashyestewa**, Herbert; m; 23 (1909); F; s; son; yes; yes; D

KUYIYOEVA

862; [Blank]; m; 59 (1874); F; m; Head; yes; yes; I
863; Belle; f; 46 (1886); F; m; wife; yes; yes; I
864; Leah; f; 26 (1906); F; s; dau; yes; yes; I
865; Willie; m; 11 (1921); F; s; son; yes; yes; I
866; Elbert; m; 7 (1925); F; s; son; yes; yes; I
867; Lela; f; 3 (9-1-28); F; s; dau; yes; yes; I

KUYONGA

868; [Blank]; f; 81 (1851); F; w; Head; yes; yes; C

KWAQUAHONEWA

869; Capitan; m; 50 (1882); F; m; Head; yes; yes; E
870; (Masivensie), Susan; f; 46 (1886); F; m; wife; yes; yes; E
871; **Talaswynema**, Lyda; f; 16 (1916); F; s; dau; yes; yes; E
872; Jewel; f; 13 (1919); F; s; dau; yes; yes; E
873; Otellio; D: 11 (1921); F; s; dau; yes; yes; E
874; Helena; f; 8 (1924); F; s; dau; yes; yes; E
875; Velta; f; 4 (11-16-27); F; s; dau; yes; yes; E

KYNAKA

876; Conner; m; 43 (1889); F; m; Head; yes; yes; E
877; Katherine; f; 50 (1882); F; m; wife; yes; yes; E
878; Ernest; m; 16 (1916); F; s; son; yes; yes; E
879; Reuben Perry; m; 14 (1918); F; s; son; yes; yes; E
880; Emery J; m; 8 (1924); F; s; son; yes; yes; E
881; **Sahme**, Olive; f; 20 (1912); F; s; stp-dau; yes; yes; E

LAEAPA

882; Elizabeth; f; 38 (1894); F; w; Head; yes; yes; A
883; Leo Crane; m; 20 (1912); F; s; son; yes; yes; A

KEY: Census Number; Name; Sex; Age at Last Birthday; Tribe (Hopi, unless otherwise stated); Degree of Blood; Marital Status; Relationship to Head of Family; At Jurisdiction where enrolled [Yes or No] (If no, Where); Ward [Yes or No]; Hopi Village [according to key].

884; Mary Inez; f; 16 (1916); F; s; dau; yes; yes; A
885; Coredelia; f; 13 (1919); F; s; dau; yes; yes; A
886; Geraldine; f; 10 (1922); F; s; dau; yes; yes; A
887; Alberta; f; 4 (4-1-28); F; s; dau; yes; yes; A
888; Bennett; m; 1 (2-6-31); F; s; son; yes; yes; A

LAHPOO

889; Jean; m; 44 (1888); F; m; Head; yes; yes; A
890; Edith; f; 38 (1894); F; m; wife; yes; yes; A
891; Cornelia; f; 16 (1916); F; s; dau; yes; yes; A
892; Edith Irene; f; 11 (1921); F; s; dau; yes; yes; A
893; Atlanta; f; 9 (1923); F; s; dau; yes; yes; A
894; Florence; f; 4 (3-3-28); F; s; dau; yes; yes; A
895; Marie; f; 1 (6-13-30); F; s; dau; yes; yes; A

LELATSE

896; [Blank]; m; 62 (1870); F; w; Head; yes; yes; B
897; Lucille; f; 11 (1921); F; s; dau; yes; yes; B
898; Mildred; f; 9 (1923); F; s; dau; yes; yes; B
899; Ruth; f; 8 (1924); F; s; dau; yes; yes; B

LALE

900; Alfred; m; 29 (1903); F; m; Head; yes; yes; B
901; Elsie; f; 31 (1901); F; m; wife; yes; yes; B
902; Pearl; f; 5 (1927); F; s; dau; yes; yes; B
903; Claud; m; 3 (1929); F; s; son; yes; yes; B

904; [Blank]; m; 62 (1870); F; m; Head; yes; yes; B
905; Lucy; f; 60 (1872); F; m; wife; yes; yes; B
906; Raymond; m; 25 (1907); F; s; son; yes; yes; B
907; Germaine; f; 19 (1913); F; s; dau; yes; yes; B
908; Ella; f; 16 (1916); F; s; dau; yes; yes; B
909; Eric; m; 13 (1918); F; s; son; yes; yes; B

LANSA

910; John; m; 31 (1901); F; m; Head; yes; yes; G
911; Mina; f; 28 (1904); F; m; wife; yes; yes; G
912; May; f; 5 (4-30-28); F; s; dau; yes; yes; G
913; Betty; f; 4 (9-29-27); F; s; dau; yes; yes; G
914; June; f; 3 (9-1-29) F; s; dau; yes; yes; G

KEY: Census Number; Name; Sex; Age at Last Birthday; Tribe (Hopi, unless otherwise stated); Degree of Blood; Marital Status; Relationship to Head of Family; At Jurisdiction where enrolled [Yes or No] (If no, Where); Ward [Yes or No]; Hopi Village [according to key].

915; Edward; m; 1(2-12-31); F; s; son; yes; yes; G

LASSES

916; [Blank]; m; 55 (1877); F; w; Head; yes; yes; B
917; Clarence; m; 24 (1908); F; s; son; yes; yes; B

LATIOM

918; [Blank]; m; 86 (1846); F; w; Head; yes; yes; C
919; Ralph; m; 36 (1896); F; s; son; yes; yes; C

LESLIE

920; Finny; m; 31 (1901); F; m; Head; yes; yes; C
921; Ruth; f; 25 (1907); F; m; wife; yes; yes; C
922; Hester; f; 3 (4-10-28); F; s; dau; yes; yes; C
923; Cynthia; f; 1 (6-1-30); F; s; dau; yes; yes; C

LESSO

924; Nampeyo; f; 64 (1868); F; w; Head; yes; yes; A

925; Wesley; m; 32 (1900); F; m; Head; yes; yes; A
926; Eloise; f; 5 (5-2-26); F; s; dau; yes; yes; A
927; Wesley, Jr; m; 3 (1929); F; s; son; yes; yes; A

LILEOKANG

928; Claude; m; 32 (1900); F; m; Head; yes; yes; I
929; Evelyn; f; 37 (1895); F; m; wife; yes; yes; I

LOLOMA

930; [Blank]; m; 35 (1897); F; m; Head; yes; yes; I
931; Rachael; f; 29 (1903); F; m; wife; yes; yes; I
932; Charles; m; 10 (1922); F; s; son; yes; yes; I
933; Peggy; f; 7 (1925); F; s; dau; yes; yes; I
934; Letitia; f; 4 (1927); F; s; dau; yes; yes; I
935; **Gashquaptewa**, Mark; m; 22 (1910); F; s; bro-in-law; yes; yes; I
936; **Koyungwytewa**, [Blank]; m; 58 (1874); F; s; uncle; yes; yes; I

HOPI INDIAN CENSUS, (As of April 1, 1932)

KEY: Census Number; Name; Sex; Age at Last Birthday; Tribe (Hopi, unless otherwise stated); Degree of Blood; Marital Status; Relationship to Head of Family; At Jurisdiction where enrolled [Yes or No] (If no, Where); Ward [Yes or No]; Hopi Village [according to key].

LOLOMAYUMA

937; [Blank]; m; ?; F; m; Head; yes; yes; F
938; Loretta; f; ?; F; m; wife; yes; yes; F
939; Jacob; m; 26 (1906); F; s; son; yes; yes; F
940; Robert; m; 20 (1912); F; s; son; yes; yes; F
941; Victor; m; 10 (1922); F; s; son; yes; yes; F
942; **Kabotie**, Fred; m; 32 (1900); F; s; nephew; yes; yes; F

LOLONGYUMA

943; [Blank]; m; 89 (1843); F; w; Head; yes; yes; F

LOLAYESTEWA

944; Ned; m; 38 (1894); F; m; Head; yes; yes; F
945; Ada Brady; f; 39 (1893); F; m; wife; yes; yes; F
946; Constance; f; 16 (1916); F; s; dau; yes; yes; F
947; Clarence; m; 9 (1923); F; s; son; yes; yes; F
948; Illa; f; 9 (1924); F; s; dau; yes; yes; F
949; Luella; f; 5 (6-26-26); F; s; dau; yes; yes; F
950; **Lowayyesie**, Oleta; f; 63 (1869); F; w; mother-in-law; yes; yes; F

LOMACOOYEVA

951; Jackson; m; 60 (1872); F; m; Head; yes; yes; H
952; Ida; f; 59 (1873); F; m; wife; yes; yes; H

LOMAHEFTEWA

953; Viets; m; 35 (1897); F; m; Head; yes; yes; F
954; Helen; f; 37 (1895); F; m; wife; yes; yes; F
955; Val Jean; m; 16 (1916); F; s; son; yes; yes; F
956; Alonzo; m; 15 (1917); F; s; son; yes; yes; F
957; Clifford; m; 12 (1920); F; s; son; yes; yes; F
958; Lola; f; 9 (1923); F; s; dau; yes; yes; F
959; Henry; m; 5 (1927); F; s; son; yes; yes; F
960; Anna; f; 3 (3-15-29); F; s; dau; yes; yes; F
961; **Kewanuyma**, Silas; m; 53 (1879); F; w; uncle; yes; yes; F

LOMAHEPTEWA

962; Roy; m; 39 (1893); F; m; Head; yes; yes; I
963; Anna; f; 33 (1899); F; m; wife; yes; yes; I

37

KEY: Census Number; Name; Sex; Age at Last Birthday; Tribe (Hopi, unless otherwise stated); Degree of Blood; Marital Status; Relationship to Head of Family; At Jurisdiction where enrolled [Yes or No] (If no, Where); Ward [Yes or No]; Hopi Village [according to key].

964; Effie; f; 14 (1918); F; s; dau; yes; yes; I
965; Calvin Coolidge; m; 10 (1922); F; s; son; yes; yes; I
966; Carroll; m; 3 (6-27-28); F; s; son; yes; yes; I
967; Mark; m; ?; F; s; son; yes; yes; I

KOYAHONSIE*

968; [Blank]; f; 72 (1860); F; w; Head; yes; yes; I

[*NOTE: Spelled as is on original census]

LOMAHVENTEWA

969; [Blank]; m; 66 (1866); F; m; Head; yes; yes; A
970; Tahwomana; f; 64 (1868); F; m; wife; yes; yes; A
971; Clifford; m; 35 (1897); F; s; son; yes; yes; A
972; Earl; m; 28 (1904); F; s; son; yes; yes; A

LOMAKEMA

973; Jackson; m; 37 (1895); F; m; Head; yes; yes; C
974; Imogene; f; 31 (1901); F; m; wife; yes; yes; C
975; Jeannette; f; 11 (1921); F; s; dau; yes; yes; C
976; Roderick; m; 7 (1925); F; s; son; yes; yes; C
977; Stetson; m; 4 (3-25-28); F; s; son; yes; yes; C
978; Luther; m; 1 (11-11-1930); F; s; son; yes; yes; C

979; [Blank]; m; 68 (1864); F; m; Head; yes; yes; F
980; Sarah; f; 66 (1866); F; m; wife; yes; yes; F
981; Charles; m; 22 (1910); F; s; son; yes; yes; F

LOMAKIARO

982; Paul; m; 39 (1894); F; m; Head; yes; yes; D
983; (Kewanhonema), Jane; f; 39 (1894); F; m; wife; yes; yes; D
984; **Nichols**, Neva; f; 16 (1916); F; s; dau; yes; yes; D

LOMANAKOSA

985; [Blank]; m; 79 (1855); F; m; Head; yes; yes; I
986; (Koeyabe), [Blank]; f; 69 (1863); F; m; wife; yes; yes; I

KEY: Census Number; Name; Sex; Age at Last Birthday; Tribe (Hopi, unless otherwise stated); Degree of Blood; Marital Status; Relationship to Head of Family; At Jurisdiction where enrolled [Yes or No] (If no, Where); Ward [Yes or No]; Hopi Village [according to key].

LOMANAQUIESSA

987; [Blank]; m; 57 (1875); F; m; Head; yes; yes; C
988; Tahlawinka; f; 58 (1874); F; m; wife; yes; yes; C

LOMANGAYTEWA

989; [Blank]; m; 82 (1850); F; w; Head; yes; yes; I

LOMANHE

990; Donald; m; 27 (1905); F; m; Head; yes; yes; D
991; Elinor Barbara; f; 6 (1926); F; s; dau; yes; yes; D

LOMANIKEOMA

992; Chris; m; 70 (1862); F; m; Head; yes; yes; D
993; (Quavemsie), [Blank]; f; 65 (1867); F; m; wife; yes; yes; D
994; **Yulatseoma**, Sidney; m; 24 (1908); F; s; son; yes; yes; D

LOMANONTIWA

995; [Blank]; m; 63 (1869); F; w; Head; yes; yes; G
996; Max; m; 30 (1901); F; s; son; yes; yes; G
997; Elie; m; 25 (1907); F; s; son; yes; yes; G
998; Francis; m; 17 (1915); F; s; son; yes; yes; G

LOMANUXSU

999; [Blank]; m; 65(1867); F; m; Head; yes; yes; D
1000; (Kwahongaema), [Blank]; f; 48 (1884); F; m; wife; yes; yes; D
1001; **Sewsnuh**, Hubert; m; 44 (1889); F; s; bro-in-law; yes; yes; D
1002; **Nanwestewa**, [Blank]; m; 56 (1876); F; w; bro-in-law; yes; yes; D
1003; **Bahnee**, Eugene; m; 20 (1912); F; s; stp-nephew; yes; yes; D

LOMAQUAU

1004; [Blank]; m; 48 (1884); F; m; Head; yes; yes; I
1005; Verla; f; 51 (1881); F; m; wife; yes; yes; I
1006; Clarence; m; 20 (1912); F; s; son; yes; yes; I
1007; Percy; m; 18 (1914); F; s; son; yes; yes; I
1008; Bonnie; f; 15 (1917); F; s; dau; yes; yes; I
1009; Lillian; f; 11 (1921); F; s; dau; yes; yes; I
1010; Luanna; f; 9 (1923); F; s; dau; yes; yes; I

KEY: Census Number; Name; Sex; Age at Last Birthday; Tribe (Hopi, unless otherwise stated); Degree of Blood; Marital Status; Relationship to Head of Family; At Jurisdiction where enrolled [Yes or No] (If no, Where); Ward [Yes or No]; Hopi Village [according to key].

1011; John; m; 4 (3-29-28); F; s; son; yes; yes; I

LOMASINGYONGWA

1012; Mike; m; 61 (1871); F; m; Head; yes; yes; F
1013; Charlotte; f; 73 (1859); F; m; wife; yes; yes; F

LOMASNEWA

1014; Gretta; f; 53 (1879); F; m; Head; yes; yes; F
1015; **Ewanheptwa**, Jay; m; 50 (1882); F; m; hus; yes; yes; F
1016; Boyd; m; 19 (1913); F; s; son; yes; yes; F

1017; Jason; m; 29 (1903); F; m; Head; yes; yes; F
1018; Laurene; f; 6 (1926); F; s; dau; yes; yes; F

LOMAVITA

1019; Otto; m; 36 (1896); F; m; Head; yes; yes; G
1020; Maybelle; f; 34 (1898); F; m; wife; yes; yes; G
1021; Timothy; m; 13 (1919); F; s; son; yes; yes; G
1022; Margaret; f; 12 (1920); F; s; dau; yes; yes; G
1023; Louise; f; 8 (1924); F; s; dau; yes; yes; G
1024; Alvin D: m; 4 (3-25-28); F; s; son; yes; yes; G

LOMAVOYA

1025; George; m; 55 (1877); F; w; Head; yes; yes; B
1026; Juanita; f; 29 (1903); F; s; dau; yes; yes; B
1027; Lawrence; m; 25 (1907); F; s; son yes; yes; B

LOMAVUYAWMA

1028; [Blank]; m; 91 (1841); F; m; Head; yes; yes; G
1029; Tahresa; f; 84 (1848); F; m; wife; yes; yes; G
1030; Curay; m; 21 (1911); F; s; grnd-son; yes; yes; G
1031; Frank; m; 20 (1912); F; s; grnd-son; yes; yes; G
1032; Conard[sic]; m; 25 (1907); F; s; grnd-son; yes; yes; G
1033; Zella; f; 18 (1914); F; s; grnd-dau; yes; yes; G
1034; Vera; f; 17 (1915); F; s; grnd-dau; yes; yes; G
1035; Majil; f; 16 (1916); F; s; grnd-dau; yes; yes; G
1036; Floyd; m; 15 (1917); F; s; grnd-son; yes; yes; G

KEY: Census Number; Name; Sex; Age at Last Birthday; Tribe (Hopi, unless otherwise stated); Degree of Blood; Marital Status; Relationship to Head of Family; At Jurisdiction where enrolled [Yes or No] (If no, Where); Ward [Yes or No]; Hopi Village [according to key].

LOMAYESVA

1037; Fred; m; 30 (1902); F; m; Head; yes; yes; G
1038; Martha; f; 31 (1901); F; m; wife; yes; yes; G
1039; Reuben; m; 12 (1920); F; s; son; yes; yes; G
1040; June; f; 9 (1923); F; s; dau; yes; yes; G
1041; Jonathan; m; 7 (1925); F; s; son; yes; yes; G
1042; Bernice; f; 5 (10-5-26); F; s; dau; yes; yes; G
1043; Ruth; f; 2 (10-5-29); F; s; dau; yes; yes; G
1044; Fern; f; 1/12 (2-9-32); F; s; dau; yes; yes; G

1045; Jasper; m; 56 (1874); F; m; Head; yes; yes; G
1046; Clara; f; 43 (1889); F; m; wife; yes; yes; G
1047; Louis; m; 17 (1915); F; s; son; yes; yes; G
1048; Helena; f; 13 (1919); F; s; dau; yes; yes; G
1049; May; f; 10 (1922); F; s; dau; yes; yes; G
1050; Mary; f; 1 (12-10-30); F; s; dau; yes; yes; G

LOMIYOWMA

1051; [Blank]; m; 83 (1849); F; m; Head; yes; yes; I
1052; Coyaminim; f; 79 (1853); F; m; wife; yes; yes; I

LOMIYUMPTEWA

1053; [Blank]; m; 60 (1872); F; m; Head; yes; yes; B
1054; (Kutahongsis), [Blank]; f; 55 (1877); F; m; wife; yes; yes; B

LOMOURIE

1055; Glenn; m; 51 (1881); F; m; Head; yes; yes; E
1056; (Honinema), Nina; f; 47 (1885); F; m; wife; yes; yes; E

LOMOYESVA

1057; George; m; 58 (1874); F; m; Head; yes; yes; B
1058; Myra; f; 59 (1873); F; m; wife; yes; yes; B
1059; Shankey; m; 19 (1913); F; s; son; yes; yes; B
1060; Imogene; f; 17 (1915); F; s; dau; yes; yes; B

LOWLOWEE

1061; Carrol; m; 32 (1900); F; m; Head; yes; yes; I
1062; Judith; f; 28 (1904); F; m; wife; yes; yes; I

KEY: Census Number; Name; Sex; Age at Last Birthday; Tribe (Hopi, unless otherwise stated); Degree of Blood; Marital Status; Relationship to Head of Family; At Jurisdiction where enrolled [Yes or No] (If no, Where); Ward [Yes or No]; Hopi Village [according to key].

MACHTO

1063;   [Blank]; m; 75 (1857); F; w; Head; yes; yes; C

MACKET

1064;   Virginia; f; 31 (1901); F; m; Head; yes; yes; G
1065;   Rolland; m; 11 (1921); F; s; son; yes; yes; G
1066;   Bella May; f; 10 (1922); F; s; dau; yes; yes; G

MAHAPE

1067;   Carl; m; 38 (1894); F; m; Head; yes; yes; I
1068;   Patty; f; 32 (1900); F; m; wife; yes; yes; I
1069;   Letha; f; 7 (1925); F; s; dau; yes; yes; I
1070;   Albert; m; 2 (1930); F; s; son; yes; yes; I
1071;   George; m; 11/12 (5-1-31); F; s; son; yes; yes; I

MAHCHEOMA

1072;   [Blank]; m; 56 (1876); F; s; Head; yes; yes; C

MAHHO

1073;   [Blank]; m; 59 (1873); F; m; Head; yes; yes; C
1074;   Kooye; f; 55 (1877); F; m; wife; yes; yes; C
1075;   Mary Louise; f; 18 (1914); F; s; niece; yes; yes; C
1076;   Davis; m; 9 (1923); F; s; son; yes; yes; C

MAHKEWA

1077;   (Chapella), Grace; f; 44 (1888); F; w; Head; yes; yes; A
1078;   Donald; m; 21 (1911); F; s; son; yes; yes; A
1079;   Alma; f; 17 (1915); F; s; dau; yes; yes; A
1080;   **Dache**, Dennis; m; 21 (1911); F; s; nephew; yes; yes; A
1081;   **Dache**, Grace; f; 15 (1917); F; s; niece; yes; yes; A
1082;   **Dache**, Mary C; f; 13 (1919); F; s; niece; yes; yes; A

MAHLE

1083;   Travis; m; 42 (1890); F; m; Head; yes; yes; A
1084;   Dell; f; 37 (1895); F; m; wife; yes; yes; A
1085;   Otis; m; 19 (1913); F; s; son; yes; yes; A
1086;   John H; m; 12 (1920); F; s; son; yes; yes; A

KEY: Census Number; Name; Sex; Age at Last Birthday; Tribe (Hopi, unless otherwise stated); Degree of Blood; Marital Status; Relationship to Head of Family; At Jurisdiction where enrolled [Yes or No] (If no, Where); Ward [Yes or No]; Hopi Village [according to key].

1087; Kendrick; m; 8 (1924); F; s; son; yes; yes; A
1088; Chester; m; 3 (5-24-28); F; s; son; yes; yes; A
1089; Verla; f; 1 (5-16-30); F; s; dau; yes; yes; A

MAHO

1090; Wallace; m; 31 (1901); F; m; Head; yes; yes; D
1091; Dora; f; 31 (1901); F; m; wife; yes; yes; D
1092; Susie; f; 10 (1922); F; s; dau; yes; yes; D
1093; Lynette; f; 9 (1924); F; s; dau; yes; yes; D
1094; Bertha K; f; 6 (1926); F; s; dau; yes; yes; D
1095; Benjamin; m; 3 (5-30-28); F; s; son; yes; yes; D

MAHEAHNIMKA

1096; [Blank]; f; 85 (1847); F; w; Head; yes; yes; C
1097; Selma; f; 53 (1979); F; s; dau; yes; yes; C

MAHAWONGNE

1098; Mutz; m; 66 (1866); F; m; Head; yes; yes; A
1099; Ada; f; 39 (1893); F; m; wife; yes; yes; A
1100; Karl; m; 13 (1919); F; s; son; yes; yes; A
1101; Ada Lee; f; 9 (1923); F; s; dau; yes; yes; A
1102; Thania; f; 2 (11-5-29); F; s; dau; yes; yes; A

MAKEWA

1103; John; m; 52 (1880); F; s; Head; yes; yes; E

MANSFIELD

1104; Louis; m; 31 (1901); F; m; Head; yes; yes; C

MASAHONVA

1105; [Blank]; m; 71 (1861); F; m; Head; yes; yes; G
1106; Solimana; f; 67 (1865); F; m; wife; yes; yes; G
1107; Edward; m; 47 (1885); F; m; son; yes; yes; G

MASAKWAPTIWA

1108; [Blank]; m; 55 (1877); F; w; Head; yes; yes; G
1109; Genevieve; f; 11 (1921); F; s; dau; yes; yes; G

43

KEY: Census Number; Name; Sex; Age at Last Birthday; Tribe (Hopi, unless otherwise stated); Degree of Blood; Marital Status; Relationship to Head of Family; At Jurisdiction where enrolled [Yes or No] (If no, Where); Ward [Yes or No]; Hopi Village [according to key].

1110; Elma; f; 8 (1924); F; s; dau; yes; yes; G

MASAQUAPTEWA

1111; Herman; m; 45 (1887); F; m; Head; yes; yes; H
1112; Susie; f; 45 (1887); F; m; wife; yes; yes; H
1113; Rachael; f; 17 (1915); F; s; dau; yes; yes; H
1114; Eldridge; m; 14 (1918); F; s; son; yes; yes; H

MASATEWA

1115; [Blank]; m; 86 (1846); F; m; Head; yes; yes; I
1116; Kootswysie; f; 72 (1860); F; m; wife; yes; yes; I

MASAVIEMA

1117; [Blank]; m; 78 (1854); F; m; Head; yes; yes; G
1118; Quomana; f; 78 (1854); F; m; wife; yes; yes; G

MASAWISTEWA

1119; [Blank]; m; 57 (1875); F; m; Head; yes; yes; G
1120; Myrtle; f; 59 (1873); F; m; wife; yes; yes; G
1121; Chester; m; 25 (1807); F; s; son; yes; yes; G
1122; Evelyn; f; 19 (1913); F; s; dau; yes; yes; G
1123; Ella; f; 17 (1915); F; s; dau; yes; yes; G
1124; George; m; 15 (1917); F; s; son; yes; yes; G

MASAYANTIWA

1125; Harry; m; 32 (1900); F; m; Head; yes; yes; G
1126; Nettie; f; 29 (1903); F; m; wife; yes; yes; G
1127; May; f; 8 (1924); F; s; dau; yes; yes; G
1128; Ellen; f; 3 (6-12-28); F; s; dau; yes; yes; G
1129; Lois; f; 1 (4-24-30); F; s; dau; yes; yes; G

MASAYESVA

1130; Albert; m; 48 (1884); F; m; Head; yes; yes; D
1131; (Kasnimpka), Miriah; f; 47 (1885); F; m; wife; yes; yes; D
1132; **Talahongse**, Anise; f; 17 (1915); F; s; dau; yes; yes; D
1133; Cortez; m; 14 (1918); F; s; son; yes; yes; D
1134; Viola; f; 9 (1925); F; s; dau; yes; yes; D
1135; Ella Mae; f; 7 (1925); F; s; dau; yes; yes; D

KEY: Census Number; Name; Sex; Age at Last Birthday; Tribe (Hopi, unless otherwise stated); Degree of Blood; Marital Status; Relationship to Head of Family; At Jurisdiction where enrolled [Yes or No] (If no, Where); Ward [Yes or No]; Hopi Village [according to key].

1136; Lorain; f; 4 (1928); F; s; dau; yes; yes; D
1137; **Ooewa**, [Blank]; m; 65 (1867); F; w; father-in-law; yes; yes; D

MASAYUMPTEWA

1138; [Blank]; m; 56 (1876); F; m; Head; yes; yes; I
1139; (Kewanesie), [Blank]; f; 56 (1877); F; m; wife; yes; yes; I

MASHANGOTEWA

1140; [Blank]; m; 57 (1875); F; m; Head; yes; yes; I
1141; (Hoenimka), [Blank]; f; 55 (1877); F; m; wife; yes; yes; I
1142; **Holemah**, Asa; m; 23 (1909); F; s; stp-son; yes; yes; I
1143; **Sockinima**, Ira; m; 17 (1915); F; s; stp-son; yes; yes; I
1144; **Tuvahongeoma**, Jefferson; m; 13 (1919); F; s; stp-son; yes; yes; I

MASHINGNEWA

1145; [Blank]; m; 58 (1874); F; w; Head; yes; yes; H
1146; Isaac; m; 21 (1911); F; s; son; yes; yes; H

MASIYESVA

1147; [Blank]; m; 53 (1879); F; m; Head; yes; yes; H
1148; Tuvahoinim; f; 54 (1878); F; m; wife; yes; yes; H
1149; Mary; f; 23 (1909); F; s; dau; yes; yes; H
1150; Tyler; m; 20 (1912); F; s; son; yes; yes; H
1151; Victor; m; 17 (1915); F; s; son; yes; yes; H
1152; Polly; f; 10 (1922); F; s; dau; yes; yes; H
1153; Ezra; m; 7 (1925); F; s; son; yes; yes; H

MASKEEF

1154; Jefferson; m; 37 (1895); F; m; Head; yes; yes; G
1155; Cora; f; 29 (1903); F; m; wife; yes; yes; G
1156; Florence; f; 9 (1924); F; s; dau; yes; yes; G
1157; Catherine; f; 5 (3-15-27); F; s; dau; yes; yes; G
1158; Ivan; m; 3 (1929); F; s; son; yes; yes; G
1159; Emma; f; 1 (2-25-31); F; s; dau; yes; yes; G

MASSAH

1160; [Blank]; m; 47 (1885); F; s; Head; yes; yes; C

HOPI INDIAN CENSUS, (As of April 1, 1932)

KEY: Census Number; Name; Sex; Age at Last Birthday; Tribe (Hopi, unless otherwise stated); Degree of Blood; Marital Status; Relationship to Head of Family; At Jurisdiction where enrolled [Yes or No] (If no, Where); Ward [Yes or No]; Hopi Village [according to key].

MASSANIMPTEWA

1161; Simon; m; 31 (1901); F; m; Head; yes; yes; I
1162; Josephine; f; 28 (1904); F; m; wife; yes; yes; I
1163; Ralph; m; 10 (1922); F; s; son; yes; yes; I
1164; Lena; f; 7 (1925); F; s; dau; yes; yes; I
1165; Maxine; f; 4 (3-16-28); F; s; dau; yes; yes; I
1166; Mollie; f; 1 (10-1-30); f; s; dau; yes; yes; I

MATSWA

1167; Wilfred; m; 45 (1887); F; m; Head; yes; yes; A
1168; Ethel; f; 40 (1892); F; m wife; yes; yes; A
1169; Clifford; m; 9 (1923); F; s; son; yes; yes; A
1170; Vivien; f; 8/12 (8-10-31); F; s; dau; yes; yes; A

MIHPI

1171; [Blank]; m; 50 (1882); F; m; Head; yes; yes; C
1172; Rita; f; 49 (1883); F; m; wife; yes; yes; C
1173; Moffitt; m; 19 (1913); F; s; son; yes; yes; C
1174; Ebin; m; 14 (1918); F; s; son; yes; yes; C

MOCKTA

1175; Alden; m; 44 (1888); F; m; Head; yes; yes; I
1176; Carrie; f; 42 (1890); F; m; wife; yes; yes; I
1177; Russell; m; 15 (1917); F; s; son; yes; yes; I
1178; Lottie; f; 12 (1920); F; s; dau; yes; yes; I
1179; Louise; f; 1 (1950); F; s; dau; yes; yes; I

MOCKTIMA

1180; Guy; m; ?; F; m; Head; yes; yes; I
1181; Amelia; f; ?; F; m; wife; yes; yes; I
1182; Lorien; m; 11 (1921); F; s; son; yes; yes; I
1183; Willard; m; 2 (4-28-29); F; s; son; yes; yes; I

MONNONGE

1184; David; m; 34 (1898); F; m; Head; yes; yes; I
1185; Nora; f; 30 (1902); F; m; wife; yes; yes; I
1186; Olive; f; 12 (1920); F; s; dau; yes; yes; I
1187; Lulu; f; 9 (1923); F; s; dau; yes; yes; I

KEY: Census Number; Name; Sex; Age at Last Birthday; Tribe (Hopi, unless otherwise stated); Degree of Blood; Marital Status; Relationship to Head of Family; At Jurisdiction where enrolled [Yes or No] (If no, Where); Ward [Yes or No]; Hopi Village [according to key].

1188; McNeil; m; 7 (1825); F; s; son; yes; yes; I
1189; Catherine Dolly; f; 2 (3-1-30); F; s; dau; yes; yes; I

MOOCHTEWA

1190; Gilbert; m; 30 (1902); F; m; Head; yes; yes; A
1191; Irene; f; 27 (1905); F; m; wife; yes; yes; A
1192; Bernard; m; 2 (3-31-30); F; s; son; yes; yes; A

MOOTAKA

1193; Tommy; m; 58 (1874); F; m; Head; yes; yes; G
1194; Alice; f; 53 (1879); F; m; wife; yes; yes; G
1195; Waldo; m; 22 (1910); F; s; son; yes; yes; G
1196; Norma; f; 12 (1920); F; s; dau; yes; yes; G
1197; Alberta; f; 11 (1921); F; s; dau; yes; yes; G

NAAZEWA

1198; Earl; m; 35 (1897); F; m; Head; yes; yes; B
1199; Vivian; f; 27 (1905); F; m; wife; yes; yes; B

NAHA

1200; Ada; f; 28 (1904); F; w; Head; yes; yes; B
1201; Myra; f; 10 (1922); F; s; dau; yes; yes; B
1202; Beulah; f; 7 (1925); F; s; dau; yes; yes; B

1203; Charley; m; 35 (1897); F; m; Head; yes; yes; B
1204; Lulu; f; 34 (1898); F; m; wife; yes; yes; B

1205; Neal; m; 24 (1908); F; m; Head; yes; yes; A
1206; Daisy; f; 27 (1905); F; m; wife; yes; yes; A
1207; Ray; m; 2 (1205029); F; s; son; yes; yes; A
1208; William Albert; m; 1 (5-30-30); F; s; son; yes; yes; A

1209; Paquah; f; 48 (1884); F; w; Head; yes; yes; A
1210; Virginia; f; 26 (1906); F; s; dau; yes; yes; A
1211; Archie; m; 18 (1914); F; s; son; yes; yes; A
1212; Emory K; m; 16 (1916); F; s; son; yes; yes; A
1213; Joy Hope; f; 14 (1918); F; s; dau; yes; yes; A

1214; Vinton; m; 33 (1899); F; s; Head; yes; yes; B

KEY: Census Number; Name; Sex; Age at Last Birthday; Tribe (Hopi, unless otherwise stated); Degree of Blood; Marital Status; Relationship to Head of Family; At Jurisdiction where enrolled [Yes or No] (If no, Where); Ward [Yes or No]; Hopi Village [according to key].

1215; King; m; 30 (1902); F; m; Head; yes; yes; B
1216; Mattie; f; 25 (1907); F; m; wife; yes; yes; B
1217; Josephine; f; 4 (1-10-28); F; s; dau; yes; yes; B
1218; Albert Vincent; m; 2; (1930); F; s; son; yes; yes; B
1219; Emerson; m; 3/12 (1-31-32); F; s; son; yes; yes; B

NAHE

1220; Samuel; m; 33 (1899); F; m; Head; yes; yes; B
1221; Lucy; f; 30 (1902); F; m; wife; yes; yes; B
1222; Grace; f; 7 (1925); F; s; dau; yes; yes; B
1223; Ruth; f; 5 (1927); F; s; dau; yes; yes; B
1224; Pat; m; 3 (1929); F; s; son; yes; yes; B
1225; Naomi; f; 1 (6-24-30); F; s; dau; yes; yes; B

1226; [Blank]; m; 75 (1857); F; w; Head; yes; yes; B
1227; Mary; f; 35 (1897); F; s; dau; yes; yes; B
1228; Hilda; f; 28 (1904); F; s; dau; yes; yes; B
1229; Betty Miller; f; 23 (1909); F; s; dau; yes; yes; B

NAHMOKE

1230; [Blank]; m; 62 (1870); F; m; Head; yes; yes; C
1231; Lanamana; f; 60 (1872); F; m; wife; yes; yes; C
1232; Watson; m; 26 (1906); F; s; son; yes; yes; C
1233; Gibson; m; 24 (1908); F; s; son; yes; yes; C
1234; Dana; m; 21 (1911); F; s; son; yes; yes; C
1235; Maude; f; 15 (1917); F; s; dau; yes; yes; C
1236; Maxwell; m; 10 (1922)l F; son; yes; yes; C

NAHNACISSIA

1237; [Blank]; m; 56 (1876); F; m; Head; yes; yes; B
1238; Kokoma; f; 50 (1882); F; m; wife; yes; yes; B
1239; Walter Ed; m; 29 (1903); F; s; son; yes; yes; B
1240; Dean; m; 25 (1907); F; s; son; yes; yes; B

NAHOTO

1241; [Blank]; m; 62 (1870); F; m; Head; yes; yes; C
1242; Kavema; f; 60 (1872); F; m; wife; yes; yes; C

KEY: Census Number; Name; Sex; Age at Last Birthday; Tribe (Hopi, unless otherwise stated); Degree of Blood; Marital Status; Relationship to Head of Family; At Jurisdiction where enrolled [Yes or No] (If no, Where); Ward [Yes or No]; Hopi Village [according to key].

NAHQUANGNEMA

1243; Pauline; f; 61 (1871); F; s; Head; yes; yes; C

NAHSONHOYO

1244; Nash; m; 43 (1889); F; m; Head; yes; yes; B
1245; Louise; f; 38 (1894); F; m; wife; yes; yes; B
1246; Sylvia; f; 18 (1914); F; s; dau; yes; yes; B
1247; Deborah; f; 16 (1916); F; s; dau; yes; yes; B
1248; Jonathan; m; 10 (1922); F; s; son; yes; yes; B
1249; Adam; m; 8 (1924); F; s; son; yes; yes; B
1250; Julius; m; 5 (11-27-26); F; s; son; yes; yes; B
1251; Thomas; m; 3 (10-15-28); F; s; son; yes; yes; B
1252; Noel; m; 1 (10-27-30); F; s; son; yes; yes; B

NAKWAYISTIWA

1253; [Blank]; m; 69 (1863); F; m; Head; yes; yes; G
1254; Noyawaynom; f; 65 (1867); F; m; wife; yes; yes; G

NAMINGHA

1255; Emerson; m; 31 (1901); F; m; Head; yes; yes; A
1256; Rachael; f; 29 (1903); F; m; wife; yes; yes; A
1257; Priscilla; f; 8 (1924); F; s; dau; yes; yes; A
1258; Ruth; f; 5 (11-6-26); F; s; dau; yes; yes; A
1259; Dextra; f; 3 (9-7-28); F; s; dau; yes; yes; A
1260; Elinor; f; 1 (10-12-30); F; s; dau; yes; yes; A

NAMORSTIWA

1261; [Blank]; m; 32 (1900); F; s; Head; yes; yes; G

NAQUAHONGOVA

1262; [Blank]; m; 60 (1872); F; m; Head; yes; yes; E
1263; (Tuvahousie), [Blank]; f; 60 (1872); F; m; wife; yes; yes; E
1264; **Bakoyya**, George; m; 29 (1903); F; s; son; yes; yes; E
1265; **Omawatewa**, Truett; m; 19 (1913); F; s; son; yes; yes; E
1266; **Yosema**, [Blank]; m; 75 (1857); F; w; uncle; yes; yes; E

KEY: Census Number; Name; Sex; Age at Last Birthday; Tribe (Hopi, unless otherwise stated); Degree of Blood; Marital Status; Relationship to Head of Family; At Jurisdiction where enrolled [Yes or No] (If no, Where); Ward [Yes or No]; Hopi Village [according to key].

NAQUAYESVA

1267; [Blank]; m; 60 (1872); F; w; Head; yes; yes; D
1268; Lucy; f; 10 (1922); F; s; dau; yes; yes; D

NAQUAYTEWA

1269; Dan; m; 47 (1885); F; m; Head; yes; yes; D
1270; (Kawanwunima), Ora; f; 42 (1890); F; m; wife; yes; yes; D
1271; Gail; m; 6 (1926); F; s; son; yes; yes; D

NASAFTI

1272; George; m; 25 (1907); F; m; Head; yes; yes; F
1273; Dorothy; f; 27 (1905); f; m; wife; yes; yes; F
1274; Emily; f; 2 (4-24-29); F; s; dau; yes; yes; F

NASAQUAPTEWA

1275; [Blank]; m; 69 (1863); F; m; Head; yes; yes; H
1276; (Tawayanim), [Blank]; f; 69 (1863); F; m; wife; yes; yes; H
1277; Emily; f; 17 (1915); F; s; grnd-dau; yes; yes; H

NASAWOOCA

1278; [Blank]; f; 58 (1874); F; w; Head; yes; yes; H
1279; Beulah; f; 33 (1899); F; s; dau; yes; yes; H
1280; Joseph; m; 29 (1903); F; s; son; yes; yes; H
1281; Susie; f; 27 (1905); F; s; dau; yes; yes; H

NASIHONVA

1282; [Blank]; m; 58 (1874); F; m; Head; yes; yes; G
1283; Nannie; f; 50 (1882); F; m; wife; yes; yes; G
1284; Mary; f; 19 (1913); F; s; dau; yes; yes; G
1285; Lucille; f; 15 (1917); F; s; dau; yes; yes; G

NASINGYAMKA

1286; [Blank]; f; 53 (1879); F; w; Head; yes; yes; D
1287; **Hongwiseoma**, Randall; m; 25 (1907); F; s; son; yes; yes; D
1288; **Sawokya**, Carl; m; 19 (1913); F; s; son; yes; yes; D
1289; **Towahoyuma**, Stetson; m; 14 (1918); F; s; son; yes; yes; D
1290; **Kremesoema**, [Blank]; m; 59 (1873); F; w; bro; yes; yes; D

HOPI INDIAN CENSUS, (As of April 1, 1932)

KEY: Census Number; Name; Sex; Age at Last Birthday; Tribe (Hopi, unless otherwise stated); Degree of Blood; Marital Status; Relationship to Head of Family; At Jurisdiction where enrolled [Yes or No] (If no, Where); Ward [Yes or No]; Hopi Village [according to key].

1291; **Kuanhenewa**, Abraham; m; 46 (1886); F; s; bro; yes; yes; D

NASITOYNIWA

1292; [Blank]; m; 31 (1901); F; s; Head; yes; yes; G

NASIWAYTIWA

1293; [Blank]; m; 61 (1871); F; w; Head; yes; yes; G
1294; Ray; m; 35 (1897); F; s; son; yes; yes; G
1295; Harry; m; 29 (1803); F; s; son; yes; yes; G
1296; Ira; m; 23 (1809); F; s; son; yes; yes; G
1297; Carl; m; 17 (1915); F; s; son; yes; yes; G

NATWANTIWA

1298; [Blank]; m; 77 (1855); F; w; Head; yes; yes; G

NAVAKLEOMA

1299; Fritz; m; 41 (1891); F; m; Head; yes; yes; F
1300; (Takwana), Laura; f; 36 (1896); F; m; wife; yes; yes; F
1301; **Takwana**, Elwood; m; 16 (1916); F; s; stp-son; yes; yes; F
1302; **Takwana**, Harvey; m; 13 (1919); F; s; stp-son; yes; yes; F
1303; **Takwana**, Wilfred; m; 10 (1922); F; s; stp-son; yes; yes; F
1304; **Takwana**, Frederick; m; 8 (1824); F; s; stp-son; yes; yes; F
1305; **Takwana**, John; m; 6 (1926); F; s; stp-son; yes; yes; F
1306; Charlie; m; ?; F; w; father; yes; yes; F

NAVAKUKU

1307; John; m; 37 (1895); F; m; Head; yes; yes; F
1308; Lois; f; 35 (1897); F; m; wife; yes; yes; F
1309; Elma; f; 15 (1917); F; s; dau; yes; yes; F
1310; Bernice; f; 13 (1919); F; s; dau; yes; yes; F
1311; Josephine; f; 12 (1920); F; s; dau; yes; yes; F
1312; Caroline; f; 8 (1924); F; s; dau; yes; yes; F
1313; Marietta; f; 5 (8-21-26); F; s; dau; yes; yes; F
1314; LaVaun; f; 4 (1928); F; s; dau; yes; F
1315; Maryanne; f; 1(5-9-30); f; s; dau; yes; yes; F

NAVAMSA

1316; Peter; m; 37 (1895); F; m; Head; yes; yes; F

KEY: Census Number; Name; Sex; Age at Last Birthday; Tribe (Hopi, unless otherwise stated); Degree of Blood; Marital Status; Relationship to Head of Family; At Jurisdiction where enrolled [Yes or No] (If no, Where); Ward [Yes or No]; Hopi Village [according to key].

1317;   Polly; f; 26 (1906); F; m; wife; yes; yes; F
1318;   Valentine; f; 10 (1922); F; s; dau; yes; yes; F
1319;   Tyler; m; 7 (1925); F; s; son; yes; yes; F
1320;   Delores; f; 3 (1-21-29); F; s; dau; yes; yes; F
1321;   Belvera; f; 1 (11-13-30); F; s; dau; yes; yes; F

NAVASHIE

1322;   Roscoe; m; 43 (1889); F; m; Head; yes; yes; B
1323;   Agnes; f; 39 (1893); F; m; wife; yes; yes; B
1324;   Harry; m; 19 (1913); F; s; son; yes; yes; B
1325;   Josephine; f; 17 (1915); F; s; dau; yes; yes; B
1326;   Roscoe N; m; 8 (1924); F; s; son; yes; yes; B
1327;   Minnie; f; 3 (11-7-28); F; s; dau; yes; yes; B
1328;   Justin; m; 6/12 (11-13-31); F; s; son; yes; yes; B

NAYATEWA

1329;   Ned; m; 36 (1897); F; m; Head; yes; yes; B
1330;   Norma; f; 28 (1904); F; m; wife; yes; yes; B
1331;   Elizabeth; f; 8 (1924); F; s; dau; yes; yes; B
1332;   Sarah; f; 2 (7-31-29); F; s; dau; yes; yes; B
1333;   Bernice; f; 4/12 (1-16-32); F; s; dau; yes; yes; B

NEETEOMA

1334;   [Blank]; m; 67 (1865); F; m; Head; yes; yes; E
1335;   (Koniumsie), [Blank]; f; 65 (1867); F; m; wife; yes; yes; E
1336;   **Tewahmana**, Imogene; f; 20 (1912); F; s; grnd-dau; yes; yes; E
1337;   **Tanataquava**, Lee; m; 18 (1914); F; s; grnd-son; yes; yes; E
1338;   **Navawytewa**, Bernita; f; 16 (1916); F; s; grnd-dau; yes; yes; E

NEQUAPTEWA

1339;   [Blank], m; 68 (1864); F; m; Head; yes; yes; I
1340;   (Woewinka), [Blank]; f; 66 (1866); F; m; wife; yes; yes; I
1341;   **Sekahoema**, [Blank]; m; 44 (1888); F; s; son; yes; yes; I
1342;   **Tuwatsie**, [Blank]; f; 32 (1900); F; s; dau; yes; yes; I
1343;   **Tunyowsie**, Matilda; f; 24 (1908); F; s; dau; yes; yes; I
1344;   **Tuwatsie**, Calvin; m; 9 (1923); F; s; grnd-son; yes; yes; I
1345;   **Tuwatsie**, Burgess; m; 3/12 (1-2-32); F; s; grnd-son; yes; yes; I

HOPI INDIAN CENSUS, (As of April 1, 1932)

KEY: Census Number; Name; Sex; Age at Last Birthday; Tribe (Hopi, unless otherwise stated); Degree of Blood; Marital Status; Relationship to Head of Family; At Jurisdiction where enrolled [Yes or No] (If no, Where); Ward [Yes or No]; Hopi Village [according to key].

NEQUATEWA

1346; Edmonds; m; 55 (1877); F; m; Head; yes; yes; F
1347; June; f; 41 (1891); F; m; wife; yes; yes; F
1348; Nelson; m; 15 (1917); F; s; son; yes; yes; F

NETACHAAN

1349; Walter; m; 36 (1896); F; m; Head; yes; yes; B
1350; Rose; f; 36 (1896); F; m; wife; yes; yes; B
1351; Mildred; f; 14 (1918); F; s; dau; yes; yes; B
1352; Esther; f; 13 (1919); F; s; dau; yes; yes; B
1353; Walter; m; 9 (1923); F; s; son; yes; yes; B

NEVANGINEWA

1354; Bruce; m; 60 (1872); F; w; Head; yes; yes; E
1355; **Koyawventhka**, Isabelle; f; 20 (1912); F; s; dau; yes; yes; E
1356; **Quoyavema**, Riley; m; 18 (1914); F; s; son; yes; yes; E
1357; John; m; 14 (1918); F; s; son; yes; yes; E
1358; **Masakwaptewa**, Frank; m; 55 (1877); F; w; bro; yes; yes; E

NEVAYKTEWA

1359; James; m; 39 (1893); F; m; Head; yes; yes; E
1360; (Polehongeva), Beulah; f; 31 (1901); F; m; wife; yes; yes; E
1361; Dorothy; f; 12 (1920); F; s; dau; yes; yes; E
1362; Austin; m; 10 (1922); F; s; son; yes; yes; E
1363; Ella; f; 9 (1923); F; s; dau; yes; yes; E
1364; Viena; f; 1 (1-29-31); F; s; dau; yes; yes; E

NEVOUNGIATEWA

1365; Wadsworth; m; 38 (1894); F; m; Head; yes; yes; F
1366; Jill; f; 32 (1900); F; m; wife; yes; yes; F
1367; Manley; m; 15 (1917); F; s; son; yes; yes; F
1368; Edith; f; 12 (1920); F; s; dau; yes; yes; F
1369; Orvill; m; 11 (1921); F; s; son; yes; yes; F
1370; Margaret; f; 8 (1924); F; s; dau; yes; yes; F
1371; Joan; f; 6 (1926); F; s; dau; yes; yes; F
1372; Loraine; f; 4 (5-3-27); F; s; dau; yes; yes; F

KEY: Census Number; Name; Sex; Age at Last Birthday; Tribe (Hopi, unless otherwise stated); Degree of Blood; Marital Status; Relationship to Head of Family; At Jurisdiction where enrolled [Yes or No] (If no, Where); Ward [Yes or No]; Hopi Village [according to key].

NICHOLS

1373; Carl; m; ?; F; m; Head; yes; yes; I
1374; (Kewaneumptewa), Grace; f; 28 (1904); F; m; wife; yes; yes; I
1375; Mary; f; 1 (8-18-30); F; s; dau; yes; yes; I

NIPHI

1376; Henry; m; 60 (1872); F; m; Head; yes; yes; E
1377; (Bawishnema), Nannie; f; 37 (1895); F; m; wife; yes; yes; E
1378; **Polehonema**, Beth; f; 17 (1915); F; s; dau; yes; yes; E
1379; **Polehonema**, Anna; f; 14 (1918); F; s; dau; yes; yes; E
1380; Gordon; m; 11 (1921); F; s; son; yes; yes; E
1381; Henrietta; f; 4 (4-22-27); f; s; dau; yes; yes; E
1382; Herbert Hoover; m; 3 (1929); F; s; son; yes; yes; E

NOMINGAH

1383; Sidney; m; 36 (1896); F; m; Head; yes; yes; I
1384; Rebecca; f; 28 (1904); F; m; wife; yes; yes; I
1385; Annette; f; 11 (1921); F; s; dau; yes; yes; I
1386; Marshall; m; 10 (1922); F; s; son; yes; yes; I
1387; Monroe; m; 3 (1929); F; s; son; yes; yes; I
1388; Waldo; m; 3/12 (12-30-31); F; s; son; yes; yes; I

NOMSI

1389; [Blank]; m; 88 (1844); F; w; Head; yes; yes; G

NOQUAINEWA

1390; [Blank]; m; 59 (1873); F; m; Head; yes; yes; I
1391; Hume; f; 57 (1875); F; m; wife; yes; yes; I
1392; Cleo; f; 16 (1916); F; s; dau; yes; yes; I
1393; Vivian; f; 13 (1918); F; s; dau; yes; yes; I

NOQUANEMA

1394; [Blank]; m; 79 (1853); F; m; Head; yes; yes; I
1395; (Hokih), [Blank]; f; 77 (1855); F; m; wife; yes; yes; I

NOQUAPTEWA

1396; [Blank]; m; 77 (1855); F; m; Head; yes; yes; I

HOPI INDIAN CENSUS, (As of April 1, 1932)

KEY: Census Number; Name; Sex; Age at Last Birthday; Tribe (Hopi, unless otherwise stated); Degree of Blood; Marital Status; Relationship to Head of Family; At Jurisdiction where enrolled [Yes or No] (If no, Where); Ward [Yes or No]; Hopi Village [according to key].

1397; (Hermenimka), [Blank]; f; 64 (1868); F; m; wife; yes; yes; I
1398; **Davingemah**, [Blank]; m; 84 (1848); F; w; bro; yes; yes; I

NUMKEWA

1399; Owen; m; 31 (1901); F; m; Head; yes; yes; D
1400; (Polewisnema), Amy; f; 29 (1903); F; m; wife; yes; yes; D
1401; Clara Louise; f; 11 (1921); F; s; dau; yes; yes; D
1402; Dawson; m; 10 (1922); F; s; son; yes; yes; D
1403; Ethel; f; 4 (7-12-27); F; s; dau; yes; yes; D
1404; Rena; f; 2 (10-3-29); F; s; dau; yes; yes; D
1405; Harold; m; 11/12 (4-7-31); F; s; son; yes; yes; D

NUTONGULA

1406; Anthony; m; 43 (1889); F; m; Head; yes; yes; I
1407; Polehonka; f; 33 (1899); F; m; wife; yes; yes; I
1408; Madge; f; 17 (1915); F; s; dau; yes; yes; I
1409; Molly; f; 15 (1917); F; s; dau; yes; yes; I
1410; Ruth; f; 11 (1921); F; s; dau; yes; yes; I

NOTUMYA

1411; Allen; m; 32 (1900); F; m; Head; yes; yes; I
1412; Margaret; f; 31 (1901); F; m; wife; yes; yes; I
1413; Lucy; f; 13 (1919); F; s; dau; yes; yes; I
1414; Lonnie; m; 11 (1921); F; s; son; yes; yes; I
1415; Elena; f; 10 (1922); F; s; dau; yes; yes; I
1416; Peter; m; 4 (4-1-28); F; s; son; yes; yes; I
1417; Eloise; f; 1 (4-19-30); f; s; dau; yes; yes; I

OHKOWYA

1418; Lonnie; m; 37 (1895); F; m; Head; yes; yes; D
1419; Margaret; f; 33 (1899); F; m; wife; yes; yes; D
1420; Herley; m; 12 (1920); F; s; son; yes; yes; D
1421; Ross; m; 7 (1925); F; s; son; yes; yes; D
1422; Delphine; f; 1 (3-24-30); F; s; dau; yes; yes; D
1423; Evelyn; f; 1/12 (3-15-32); F; s; dau; yes; yes; D

OMAWAH

1424; [Blank]; m; 66 (1866); F; w; Head; yes; yes; B
1425; Dick; m; 30 (1902); F; s; son; yes; yes; B

55

HOPI INDIAN CENSUS, (As of April 1, 1932)

KEY: Census Number; Name; Sex; Age at Last Birthday; Tribe (Hopi, unless otherwise stated); Degree of Blood; Marital Status; Relationship to Head of Family; At Jurisdiction where enrolled [Yes or No] (If no, Where); Ward [Yes or No]; Hopi Village [according to key].

ONSAY

1426; Burton; m; 35 (1897); F; m; Head; yes; yes; F
1427; Eloise; f; 24 (1908); F; m; wife; yes; yes; F
1428; Sheila Mary; f; 5 (6-28-26); F; s; dau; yes; yes; F
1429; Lindred; m; 4 (1928); F; s; son; yes; yes; F
1430; Roland; m; 1 (3-31-31); F; s; son; yes; yes; F

OUTAH

1431; Johnny; m; 32 (1900); F; m; Head; yes; yes; A
1432; Elma; f; 27 (1905); F; m; wife; yes; yes; A
1433; George; m; 5 (11-10-26); F; s; son; yes; yes; A
1434; Corita Agnes; f; 3 (9-28-28); F; s; dau; yes; yes; A
1435; Ronald; m; 1 (12-10-30); F; s; son; yes; yes; A

1436; Victor; m; 26 (1906); F; m; Head; yes; yes; G
1437; Betty; f; 27 (1905); F; m; wife; yes; yes; G
1438; Olive; f; 5 (12-8-26); F; s; dau; yes; yes; G
1439; Leonora; f; 3/12 (12-10-31); F; s; dau; yes; yes; G

OVAH

1440; Grover; m; 55 (1877); F; m; Head; yes; yes; B
1441; Koyongenema; f; 54 (1878); F; m; wife; yes; yes; B
1442; Frances; f; 19 (1915); F; s; dau; yes; yes; B
1443; Homer; m; 17 (1915); F; s; son; yes; yes; B
1444; Berneta; f; 15 (1918); F; s; dau; yes; yes; B
1445; Paul; m; 26 (1906); F; s; son; yes; yes; B

OYAPING

1446; Nelson; m; 60 (1872); F; m; Head; yes; yes; D
1447; (Tuvahnema), Dinah; f; 40 (1892); F; m; wife; yes; yes; D
1448; **Kojaseema**, [Blank]; m; 65 (1867); F; w; father-in-law; yes; yes; D
1449; **Kwihoya**, Dick; m; 35 (1897)l F; s; bro-in-law; yes; yes; D

OYE

1450; Frank; m; 67 (1865); F; m; Head; yes; yes; A
1451; Everett; m; 36 (1894); F; w; son; yes; yes; A

56

HOPI INDIAN CENSUS, (As of April 1, 1932)

KEY: Census Number; Name; Sex; Age at Last Birthday; Tribe (Hopi, unless otherwise stated); Degree of Blood; Marital Status; Relationship to Head of Family; At Jurisdiction where enrolled [Yes or No] (If no, Where); Ward [Yes or No]; Hopi Village [according to key].

PABANALE

1452; Irving; m; 43 (1889); F; m; Head; yes; yes; A
1453; Josie; f; 39 (1893); F; m; wife; yes; yes; A
1454; Clara Belle; f; 18 (1914); F; s; dau yes; yes; A
1455; Edith; f; 9 (1923); F; s; dau; yes; yes; A

PABUSE

1456; William; m; 48 (1884); F; w; Head; yes; yes; I
1457; **Tophongnim**, Mildred; f; 29 (1903); F; m; niece; yes; yes; I
1458; **Nez**, Gertrude; f; 27 (1905); F; m; niece; yes; yes; I
1459; **Pooyohoema**, Ezra; m; 9 (1925); F; s; nephew; yes; yes; I
1460; **Pooyohoema**, Ross; m; 6 (1926); F; s; nephew; yes; yes; I
1461; **Pooyohoema**, Vera; f; ?; F; s; niece; yes; yes; I
1462; **Pooyohoema**, Myra; f; 4 (1928); F; s; niece; yes; yes; I

PAHUSEEMA

1463; [Blank]; m; 60 (1872); F; m; Head; yes; yes; D
1464; (Josevensie), Mina; f; 51 (1881); F; m; wife; yes; yes; D
1465; Allen; m; 10 (1922); F; s; son; yes; yes; D
1466; **Mofsie**, Morris; m; 26 (1907); F; s; stp-son; yes; yes; D
1467; **Koyatio**, Basil; m; 25 (1907); F; s; stp-son; yes; yes; D
1468; **Mofsie**, Frank; m; 12 (1920); F; s; stp-son; yes; yes; D
1469; **Lomatuma**, [Blank]; m; 80 (1852); F; w; father-in-law; yes; yes; D

PALAALA

1470; Robert; m; 36 (1906); F; m; Head; yes; yes; C
1471; Lucille; f; 32 (1900); F; m; wife; yes; yes; C
1472; Fred; m; 13 (1929)[sic]; F; s; son; yes; yes; C

PAVATAH

1473; Donald; m; 30 (1902); F; m; Head; yes; yes; A
1474; Polly; f; 33 (1899); F; m; wife; yes; yes; A
1475; Calvin; m; 2 (1-26-30); F; s; son; yes; yes; A

PAVATEA

1476; Theodore; m; 27 (1905); F; m; Head; yes; yes; A
1477; Genevieve; f; 24 (1908); F; m; wife; yes; yes; A
1478; Robert Lee; m; 5 (12-15-26); F; s; son; yes; yes; A

KEY: Census Number; Name; Sex; Age at Last Birthday; Tribe (Hopi, unless otherwise stated);
Degree of Blood; Marital Status; Relationship to Head of Family; At Jurisdiction where enrolled
[Yes or No] (If no, Where); Ward [Yes or No]; Hopi Village [according to key].

1479; Percy; m; 4 (2-18-28); F; s; son; yes; yes; A
1480; Schwarz; m; 3 (3-23-29); F; s; son; yes; yes; A
1481; Dick; m; 1 (6-26-30); F; s; son; yes; yes; A
1482; Virginia Quang; f; 1/12 (2-24-32); F; s; dau; yes; yes; A

1483; Tom; m; 57 (1875); F; m; Head; yes; yes; A
1484; Quang; f; 52 (1880); F; m; wife; yes; yes; A
1485; Rosetta; f; 17 (1915); F; s; dau; yes; yes; A
1486; Dorothea; f; 15 (1917); F; s; dau; yes; yes; A
1487; Tom, Jr; m; 13 (1919); F; s; son; yes; yes; A
1488; A. Womack; m; 11 (1921); F; s; son; yes; yes; A
1489; Wilhemina; f; 3 (10-25-28); F; s; dau yes; yes; A
1490; **Haeling**[sic], Percy; m; 53 (1879); F; w; bro-in-law; yes; yes; A

PAVENKA

1491; Minnie; f; 40 (1892); F; w; Head; yes; yes; D
1492; **Chevatewa**, Wilson; m; 19 (1913); F; s; son; yes; yes; D
1493; **Chevatewa**, Ray; m; 18 (1914); F; s; son; yes; yes; D
1494; **Chevatewa**, Ruth; f; 13 (1919); F; s; dau; yes; yes; D
1495; **Chevatewa**, Martha; f; 11 (1921); F; s; dau; yes; yes; D
1496; **Chevatewa**, Gerald; m; 9 (1923); F; s; son; yes; yes; D
1497; **Chevatewa**, Julia; f; 7 (1925); F; s; dau; yes; yes; D
1498; **Chevatewa**, Thelma; f; 4 (1928); F; s; dau; yes; yes; D
1499; **Chevatewa**, Susanne Rink; f; 1 (6-13-30); F; s; dau; yes; yes; D

PAWIKI

1500; Sam; m; 54 (1878); F; w; Head; yes; yes; G
1501; Lois; f; 21 (1911); F; s; dau; yes; yes; G
1502; Raymond; m; 13 (1919); F; s; son; yes; yes; G

PAHUYTEWA

1503; [Blank]; m; 54 (1878); F; m; Head; yes; yes; I
1504; (Chiseongenim), [Blank]; f; 48 (1884); F; m; wife; yes; yes; I
1505; George; m; ?; F; s; son; yes; yes; I
1506; Nellie; f; 19 (1913); F; s; dau; yes; yes; I
1507; **Mansfield**, Maggie; f; 35 (1897); F; s; niece; yes; yes; I
1508; **Mansfield**, Patricia; f; ?; F; s; gr-niece; yes; yes; I

PAYMELLA

1509; Duke; m; 44 (1886); F; w; Head; yes; yes; A

HOPI INDIAN CENSUS, (As of April 1, 1932)

KEY: Census Number; Name; Sex; Age at Last Birthday; Tribe (Hopi, unless otherwise stated); Degree of Blood; Marital Status; Relationship to Head of Family; At Jurisdiction where enrolled [Yes or No] (If no, Where); Ward [Yes or No]; Hopi Village [according to key].

1510; Ruth; f; 22 (1910); F; s; dau; yes; yes; A
1511; Robert; m; 1/1 (1)[sic]; F; s; son; yes; yes; A

PECUSA

1512; Fred; m; 58 (1874); F; m; Head; yes; yes; I
1513; Kochnika; f; 58 (1874); F; m; wife; yes; yes; I
1514; Nathan; m; 18 (1914); F; s; son; yes; yes; I

PEEPHONGOVA

1515; Joe; m; 64 (1868); F; m; Head; yes; yes; H
1516; Chozrohua; f; 62 (1870); F; m; wife; yes; yes; H
1517; Madison; m; 41 (1891); F; s; son; yes; yes; H
1518; Dorcas; f; 24 (1908); F; s; dau; yes; yes; H
1519; Carolyn; f; 22 (1910); F; s; dau; yes; yes; H

PEESAH

1520; Grant; m; 612 (1871); F; w; Head; yes; yes; B
1521; Alice; f; 19 (1913); F; s; dau; yes; yes; B
1522; Sally; f; 17 (1915); F; s; dau; yes; yes; B
1523; Herman; m; 24 (1908); F; s; son; yes; yes; B
1524; Curtis; m; 20 (1912); F; s; son; yes; yes; B
1525; Wayne; m; 9 (1923); F; s; son; yes; yes; B

PENTEWA

1526; Otto; m; 43 (1889); F; m; Head; yes; yes; G
1527; Rhoada; f; 43 (1889); F; m; wife; yes; yes; G
1528; Rowena; f; 12 (1920); F; s; dau; yes; yes; G
1529; Dick; m; 4 (4-12-27); F; s; son; yes; yes; G
1530; Fay Loray; f; 5/12 (10-29-31); F; s; dau; yes; yes; G

PEAHOKTEOMA

1531; Joab; m; 37 (1985); F; m; Head; yes; yes; E
1532; (Kemongvisie), Kitty; f; 36 (1906); F; m; wife; yes; yes; E
1533; Lawrence; m; 2 (1-13-30); F; s; son; yes; yes; E
1534; **Quemawynema**, Aubrey; f; 16 (1916); F; s; stp-dau; yes; yes; E
1535; **Quemawynema**, Gladys; f; 12 (1920); F; s; stp-dau; yes; yes; E
1536; **Lomonginewa**, Harry; m; 50 (1882); F; s; bro-in-law; yes; yes; E

HOPI INDIAN CENSUS, (As of April 1, 1932)

KEY: Census Number; Name; Sex; Age at Last Birthday; Tribe (Hopi, unless otherwise stated); Degree of Blood; Marital Status; Relationship to Head of Family; At Jurisdiction where enrolled [Yes or No] (If no, Where); Ward [Yes or No]; Hopi Village [according to key].

POEWHOEMA

1537; Nicholas; m; 50 (1882); F; m; Head; yes; yes; I
1538; Lela; f; 49 (1883); F; m; wife; yes; yes; I
1539; Imogene; f; 20 (1912); F; s; dau; yes; yes; I

POHONA

1540; Duke; m; 29 (1903); F; m; Head; yes; yes; A
1541; Edith; f; 27 (1905); F; m; wife; yes; yes; A
1542; Roberta; f; 3 (1-21-29); F; s; dau; yes; yes; A
1543; Lulu; f; 1 (3-26-31); F; s; dau; yes; yes; A

POHUMA

1544; Clyde; m; 36 (1896); F; m; Head; yes; yes; B
1545; Jane; f; 33 (1899); F; m; wife; yes; yes; B
1546; Emory K; m; 17 (1915); F; s; son; yes; yes; B
1547; Essie C; f; 15 (1917); F; s; dau; yes; yes; B
1548; Aion; m; 8 (1924); F; s; son; yes; yes; B
1549; Charlotte; f; 3 (12-2-28); F; s; dau; yes; yes; B
1550; Eva Juanita; f; 2/12 (1-8-32); F; s; dau; yes; yes; B

POLACCA

1551; Awkong; f; 71 (1861); F; w; Head; yes; yes; A

1552; Calvin; m; 33 (1899); F; w; Head; yes; yes; A
1553; Jaynes; m; 3 (5-21-28); F; s; son; yes; yes; A

1554; Clyde; m; 39 (1893); F; m; Head; yes; yes; B
1555; Barbara; f; 36 (1896); F; m; wife; yes; yes; B
1556; Kirkland; m; 14 (1918); F; s; son; yes; yes; B
1557; Rex; m; 10 (1922); F; s; son; yes; yes; B
1558; Rebecca; f; 3 (8-14-28); F; s; dau; yes; yes; B

1559; Howeta; m; 49 (1883); F; m; Head; yes; yes; A
1560; Ruth; f; 37 (1895); F; m; wife; yes; yes; A
1561; Dorothy; f; 13 (1919); F; s; dau; yes; yes; A
1562; Katherine; f; 10 (1922); F; s; dau; yes; yes; A
1563; Louise; f; 8 (1924); F; s; dau; yes; yes; A
1564; Millicent; f; 6 (1926); F; s; dau; yes; yes; A
1565; Percy; m; 4 (1928); F; s; son; yes; yes; A

KEY: Census Number; Name; Sex; Age at Last Birthday; Tribe (Hopi, unless otherwise stated); Degree of Blood; Marital Status; Relationship to Head of Family; At Jurisdiction where enrolled [Yes or No] (If no, Where); Ward [Yes or No]; Hopi Village [according to key].

1566; Kenneth; m; 25 (1907); F; m; Head; yes; yes; A
1567; Rosa Lee; f; 22 (1910); F; m; wife; yes; yes; A
1568; Christina; f; 3/12 (12-13-31); F; s; dau; yes; yes; A

1569; Starlie; m; 35 (1897); F; m; Head; yes; yes; A
1570; Elsie; f; 35 (1897); F; m; wife; yes; yes; A
1571; Wynona; f; 27 (1915); F; s; dau; yes; yes; A
1572; William Sunday; m; 15 (1917); F; s; son; yes; yes; A
1573; Corrine; f; 13 (1919); F; s; dau; yes; yes; A
1574; Starlie, Jr; m; 10 (1922); F; s; son; yes; yes; A
1575; Edith M; f; 7 (1925); F; s; dau; yes; yes; A
1576; Marian; f; 2 (11-7-29); F; s; dau; yes; yes; A
1577; Ethel Larson; f; 1/12 (3/16/32); F; s; dau; yes; yes; A

1578; Vinton; m; 30 (1902); F; m; Head; yes; yes; A
1579; Fannie; f; 29 (1903); F; m; wife; yes; yes; A
1580; Lillian B: f; 8 (1924); F; s; dau; yes; yes; A
1581; Alva; f; 6 (2-20-26); F; s; dau; yes; yes; A
1582; Leah; f; 3 (4-4-28); F; s; dau; yes; yes; A
1583; Harold; m; 2 (10-18-29); F; s; son; yes; yes; A
1584; Doran; m; 2/12 (1-16-32); F; s; son; yes; yes; A

POLEAHLA

1585; John; m; 47 (1885); F; m; Head; yes; yes; C
1586; Rose; f; 39 (1893); F; m; wife; yes; yes; C
1587; Bert; m; 18 (1914); F; s; son; yes; yes; C
1588; Evans; m; 17 (1915); F; s; son; yes; yes; C

POLEHEPTEWA

1589; [Blank]; m; 52 (1880); F; m; Head; yes; yes; H
1590; Tuvayownim; f; 49 (1883); F; m; wife; yes; yes; H
1591; Felix; m; 11 (1921); F; s; son; yes; yes; H

POLESSE

1592; [Blank]; m; 66 (1866); F; s; Head; yes; yes; B

POLEUMPTEWA

1593; [Blank]; m; 45 (1887); F; w; Head; yes; yes; I
1594; **Sekiequapnim**, [Blank]; f; 59 (1873); F; w; mother; yes; yes; I
1595; **Pahuhnim**, [Blank]; 61 (1871)[sic]; F; w; sister; yes; yes; I

61

HOPI INDIAN CENSUS, (As of April 1, 1932)

KEY: Census Number; Name; Sex; Age at Last Birthday; Tribe (Hopi, unless otherwise stated); Degree of Blood; Marital Status; Relationship to Head of Family; At Jurisdiction where enrolled [Yes or No] (If no, Where); Ward [Yes or No]; Hopi Village [according to key].

1596; **Sewehumsie**, Cora; f; 20 (1912); F; s; niece; yes; yes; I

POLVENTEWA

1597; [Blank]; m; 64 (1868); F; w; Head; yes; yes; I
1598; Cynthia; f; 20 (1912); F; s; dau; yes; yes; I

POLEWYTEWA

1599; Roscoe; m; 37 (1895); F; m; Head; yes; yes; D
1600; (Talaquafnema), Irene; f; 27 (1905); F; m; wife; yes; yes; D
1601; Harriet; f; 5 (8-9-26); F; s; dau; yes; yes; D
1602; Helen; f; 4 (9-2-27); F; s; dau; yes; yes; D
1603; Pansy; f; 2 (5-19-29); F; s; dau; yes; yes; D

POLILANEMA

1604; Otis; m; 26 (1906); F; m; Head; yes; yes; F
1605; Jessie; f; 26 (1906); F; m; wife; yes; yes; F
1606; Walter; m; 6 (2-7-26); F; s; son; yes; yes; F
1607; Lawrence; m; 3 (4-22-28); F; s; son; yes; yes; F
1608; **Hoomanifka**, Bertha; f; 55 (1988); F; w; mother-in-law; yes; yes; F
1609; **Navayumptewa**, [Blank]; m; 91 (1841); F; w; uncle; yes; yes; F

POLINGHUMPTEWA

1610; [Blank]; m; 49 (1883); F; m; Head; yes; yes; I
1611; Tawaquapnim; f; 49 (1883); F; m; wife; yes; yes; I
1612; Jack; m; 29 (1903); F; s; son; yes; yes; I
1613; Zella; f; 27 (1905); F; s; dau; yes; yes; I
1614; Simeon; m; 24 (1908); F; s; son; yes; yes; I
1615; Irene; f; 19 (1913); F; s; dau; yes; yes; I
1616; Lila; f; 17 (1915); F; s; dau; yes; yes; I
1617; Leta; f; 11 (1921); F; s; dau; yes; yes; I
1618; Stanford Hunt; m; 6 (1926); F; s; son; yes; yes; I

POLINGOWMA

1619; [Blank]; m; 55 (1877); F; m; Head; yes; yes; F
1620; Isabelle; f; 44 (1888); F; m; wife; yes; yes; F
1621; Thelma; f; 22 (1910); F; s; dau; yes; yes; F
1622; Henry; m; 12 (1920); F; s; son; yes; yes; F
1623; Gladys; f; 10 (1922); F; s; dau; yes; yes; F
1624; Tenny; m; 6 (1926); F; s; son; yes; yes; F

KEY: Census Number; Name; Sex; Age at Last Birthday; Tribe (Hopi, unless otherwise stated); Degree of Blood; Marital Status; Relationship to Head of Family; At Jurisdiction where enrolled [Yes or No] (If no, Where); Ward [Yes or No]; Hopi Village [according to key].

1625; Glenna; f; 2 (3-4-30); F; s; dau; yes; yes; F

POLINGYOHOYA

1626; Wilbur; m; 20 (1912); F; m; Head; yes; yes; F
1627; Reva; f; 22 (1910); F; m; wife; yes; yes; F
1628; Gertrude; f; 2/12 (1-7-32); F; s; dau; yes; yes; F

POLINGYAWMA

1629; [Blank]; m; ?; F; w; Head; yes; yes; G

POLIYISTIWA

1630; Dan; m; 58 (1874); F; m; Head; yes; yes; G
1631; Henrietta; f; 53 (1879); F; m; wife; yes; yes; G

POLYESTEWA

1632; King; m; 33 (1899); F; m; Head; yes; yes; F
1633; Josephine; f; 28 (1904); F; m; wife; yes; yes; F
1634; Edmond; m; 9 (1923); F; s; son; yes; yes; F
1635; Naomi; f; (1925); F; s; dau; yes; yes; F
1636; Catherine; f; 5 (2-18-27); F; s; dau; yes; yes; F
1637; Madge; f; 2 (1930); F; s; dau; yes; yes; F

PONAQUAPTEWA

1638; Otto; m; 59 (1873); F; m; Head; yes; yes; H
1639; Talashongsie; f; 61 (1871); F; m; wife; yes; yes; H
1640; Sally; f; 24 (1908); F; s; dau; yes; yes; H
1641; Ruth; f; 17 (1915); F; s; dau; yes; yes; H
1642; Silas; m; 15 (1917); F; s; son; yes; yes; H

PONAYISTIWA

1643; [Blank]; m; 63 (1869); F; m; Head; yes; yes; G
1644; Tawamansi; f; 68 (1864); F; m; wife; yes; yes; G
1645; Joseph; m; 26 (1906); F; s; son; yes; yes; G
1646; Gertie; f; 25 (1907); F; s; dau; yes; yes; G

KEY: Census Number; Name; Sex; Age at Last Birthday; Tribe (Hopi, unless otherwise stated); Degree of Blood; Marital Status; Relationship to Head of Family; At Jurisdiction where enrolled [Yes or No] (If no, Where); Ward [Yes or No]; Hopi Village [according to key].

PONCHO

1647; Juan; m; 47 (1885); F; m; Head; yes; yes; B
1648; Emma; f; 38 (1894); F; m; wife; yes; yes; B
1649; Ernest; m; 19 (1913); F; s; son; yes; yes; B
1650; Idella; f; 17 (1915); F; s; dau; yes; yes; B
1651; Harold; m; 16 (1916); F; s; son; yes; yes; B

PONYAYUMKA

1652; [Blank]; f; 63 (1869); F; w; Head; yes; yes; H
1653; **Dukave**, Bessie; f; 25 (1907); F; m; dau; yes; yes; H
1654; **Dukave**, Eric; m; 24 (1908); F; m; son-in-law; yes; yes; H
1655; **Burton**, Luella; f; 16 (1916); F; s; grnd-dau; yes; yes; H

POOCHA

1656; [Blank]; m; 64 (1868); F; m; Head; yes; yes; [village not given]
1657; Poonyounka; f; 52 (1880); F; m; wife; yes; yes; [village not given]

1658; Eldridge; m; 28 (1904); F; m; Head; yes; yes; [village not given]
1659; Joy; f; 28 (1904); f; m; wife; yes; yes; [village not given]
1660; Margie Inez; f; 2 (3-26-30); F; s; dau; yes; yes; [village not given]
1661; Malinda; f; 7/12 (8-25-31); F; s; dau; yes; yes; [village not given]

POOCHELE

1662; Dan; m; 49 (1883); F; m; Head; yes; yes; [village not given]
1663; Della; f; 29 (1903); F; m; wife; yes; yes; [village not given]
1664; Hoover; m; 11 (1921); F; s; son; yes; yes; [village not given]
1665; Bertha; f; 9 (1923); F; s; dau; yes; yes; [village not given]
1666; Millie; f; 3 (1929); F; s; dau; yes; yes; [village not given]
1667; Lettie; f; 1 (1930); F; s; dau; yes; yes; [village not given]

POOHEOHMA

1668; [Blank]; m; 58 (1874); F; m; Head; yes; yes; I
1669; Humavense; f; 57 (1875); F; m; wife; yes; yes; I

POOLA

1670; Jesse; m; 37 (1895); F; m; Head; yes; yes; C
1671; Ida Tuvy; f; 45 (1887); F; m; wife; yes; yes; C
1672; Buell; m; 10 (1928); F; s; son; yes; yes; C

64

HOPI INDIAN CENSUS, (As of April 1, 1932)

KEY: Census Number; Name; Sex; Age at Last Birthday; Tribe (Hopi, unless otherwise stated); Degree of Blood; Marital Status; Relationship to Head of Family; At Jurisdiction where enrolled [Yes or No] (If no, Where); Ward [Yes or No]; Hopi Village [according to key].

1673; Mitchell; m; 1 (3-7-31); F; s; son; yes; yes; C

POOMOSTIE

*1673; Elec; m; ?; F; m; Head; yes; yes; I
1674; Betty; f; 27 (1905); F; m; wife; yes; yes; I
1675; **Tahomana**, [Blank]; f; 87 (1845); F; w; Grnd mother; yes; yes; I
1676; **Lomannim**, Salome; f; 21 (1911); F; s; sis-in-law; yes; yes; I

[*NOTE: Same number given both times.]

POOSHOME

1677; Stanley; m; 55 (1877); F; m; Head; yes; yes; A
1678; Kelly; f; 50 (1882); F; m; wife; yes; yes; A
1679; Eleanor; f; 26 (1906); F; s; dau; yes; yes; A
1680; Carol; f; 19 (1913); F; s; dau; yes; yes; A
1681; Nancy Carol; f; 3/12 (12-28-31); F; s; grnd-dau; yes; yes; A
1682; Gertie; f; 17 (1915); F; s; dau; yes; yes; A
1683; Ruth; f; 9 (1923); F; s; dau; yes; yes; A

POOYOWMA

1684; Jean; m; 33 (1899); F; m; Head; yes; yes; A
1685; Vera; f; 33 (1899); F; m; wife; yes; yes; A
1686; Rex; m; 14 (1918); F; s; son; yes; yes; A
1687; Allen; m; 10 (1922); F; s; son; yes; yes; A
1688; Fletcher; m; 2 (8-27-1-29); F; s; son; yes; yes; A

POSEYESVA

1689; John; m; 45 (1887); F; m; Head; yes; yes; G
1690; Tressie; f; 44 (1888); F; m; wife; yes; yes; G
1691; John, Jr; m; 24 (1908); F; s; son; yes; yes; G

1692; Raymond; m; 31 (1901); F; m; Head; yes; yes; G
1693; Verna; f; 24 (1908); F; m; wife; yes; yes; G
1694; Irvin; f; 2 (12-23-29); F; s; son; yes; yes; G
1695; Pearl; f; 1 (4-1-31); F; s; dau; yes; yes; G

POSTO

1696; [Blank]; m; 84 (1848); F; m; Head; yes; yes; C
1697; Hyeh; f; 74 (1858); F; m; wife; yes; yes; C

KEY: Census Number; Name; Sex; Age at Last Birthday; Tribe (Hopi, unless otherwise stated); Degree of Blood; Marital Status; Relationship to Head of Family; At Jurisdiction where enrolled [Yes or No] (If no, Where); Ward [Yes or No]; Hopi Village [according to key].

POVOONHEYA

1698; Elmo; m; 45 (1887); F; w; Head; yes; yes; C
1699; Iver; m; 16 (1916); F; s; son; yes; yes; C

PUHUQUAPTEWA

1700; Arthur; m; 52 (1880); F; m; Head; yes; yes; H
1701; Pearl; f; 44 (1888); F; m; wife; yes; yes; H
1702; Lois; f; 16 (1915); F; s; dau; yes; yes; H

PUHUYESVA

1703; Mike; m; 39 (1893); F; m; Head; yes; yes; H
1704; Maud; f; 39 (1893); F; m; wife; yes; yes; H
1705; Pauline; f; 19 (1913); F; s; dau; yes; yes; H
1706; Eunice; f; 10 (1922); F; s; dau; yes; yes; H
1707; Hester; f; 8 (1924); F; s; dau; yes; yes; H
1708; Raymond; m; 3 (5-4-28); F; s; son; yes; yes; H
1709; **Polingyowma**, [Blank]; m; 65 (1867); F; w; father; yes; yes; H

PUKE

1710; Albert; m; 39 (1893); F; s Head; yes; yes; G

QAKWANWA

1711; Myron; m; 38 (1894); F; m; Head; yes; yes; G
1712; Grace; f; 27 (1905); F; m; wife; yes; yes; G
1713; **Navakleoma**, Lorenzo Fritz; m; 9 (1923); F; s; stp-son; yes; yes; G
1714; Lena; f; 5 (1927); F; s; stp-dau; yes; yes; G
1715; Roderick; m; 1 (3-18-31); F; s; son; yes; yes; G

QOYAYEPTIWA

1716; [Blank]; m; 94 (1838); F; w; Head; yes; yes; G

QUAHMANNA

1717; [Blank]; f; 58 (1874); F; w; Head; yes; yes; D
1718; **Sakhongova**, [Blank]; m; 60 (1872); F; w; bro; yes; yes; D

KEY: Census Number; Name; Sex; Age at Last Birthday; Tribe (Hopi, unless otherwise stated); Degree of Blood; Marital Status; Relationship to Head of Family; At Jurisdiction where enrolled [Yes or No] (If no, Where); Ward [Yes or No]; Hopi Village [according to key].

QUAHONGOVA

1719; Quentin; m; 53 (1879); F; m; Head; yes; yes; F
1720; Naomi; f; 48 (1884); F; m; wife; yes; yes; F
1721; Mildred; f; 19 (1913); F; s; dau; yes; yes; F
1722; Hastings; m; 16 (1916); F; s; son; yes; yes; F
1723; Arthur; m; 12 (1920); F; s; son; yes; yes; F
1724; Richard; m; 9 (1923); F; s; son; yes; yes; F
1725; Ruth; f; 2 (1930); F; s; dau; yes; yes; F

QUAKUKU

1726; Mancho; m; 47 (1885); F; m; Head; yes; yes; D
1727; (Sokahonsie), Kate; f; 46 (1886); F; m; wife; yes; yes; D
1728; **Lomayestewa**, Gibson; m; 18 (1914); F; s; son; yes; yes; D
1729; **Cashvamekah**, Leona; f; 16 (1916); F; s; dau; yes; yes; D

QUAMAHANKA

1730; [Blank]; f; 80 (1852); F; w; Head; yes; yes; G
1731; Tuvangayumai; f; 42 (1890); F; s; dau; yes; yes; G

1732; [Blank]; m; 69 (1863); F; m; Head; yes; yes; F
1733; Juanita; f; 42 (1890); F; m; wife; yes; yes; F
1734; Ruby; f; 17 (1915); F; s; dau; yes; yes; F
1735; Paul; m; 15 (1917); F; s; son; yes; yes; F
1736; Daniel; m; 12 (1920); F; s; son; yes; yes; F
1737; Rix; m; 9 (1923); F; s; son; yes; yes; F
1738; Rex; m; 19 (1913); F; s; grnd-son; yes; yes; F

QUAMALESTEWA

1739; Archie; m; 43 (1889); F; m; Head; yes; yes; F
1740; Nellie; f; 44 (1888); F; m; wife; yes; yes; F

QUAMANEWA

1741; Laban; m; 59 (1873); F; m; Head; yes; yes; E
1742; Omawa; f; 59 (1873); F; m; wife; yes; yes; E
1743; Lyle; m; 19 (1913); F; s; son; yes; yes; E
1744; Naomi; f; 16 (1916); F; s; dau; yes; yes; E
1745; Samuel; m; 13 (1919); F; s; son; yes; yes; E
1746; Marion; f; 10 (1922); F; s; dau; yes; yes; E
1747; Hazel; f; 8 (1924); F; s; dau; yes; yes; E

KEY: Census Number; Name; Sex; Age at Last Birthday; Tribe (Hopi, unless otherwise stated); Degree of Blood; Marital Status; Relationship to Head of Family; At Jurisdiction where enrolled [Yes or No] (If no, Where); Ward [Yes or No]; Hopi Village [according to key].

1748; Frank; m; 7 (1925); F; s; son; yes; yes; E
1749; Clara; f; 4 (3-12-28); F; s; dau; yes; yes; E

QUANIMPTEWA

1750; Lester; m; 33 (1899); F; m; Head; yes; yes; I
1751; Magdaline; f; 24 (1908); F; m; wife; yes; yes; I
1752; Harold; m; 2 (1930); F; s; son; yes; yes; I
1753; Mary Jane; f; 1 (1931); F; s; dau; yes; yes; I

QUANNE

1754; Horace; m; 38 (1894); F; m; Head; yes; yes; G
1755; Jennie; f; 39 (1893); F; m; wife; yes; yes; G
1756; Rebecca; f; 21 (1911); F; s; dau; yes; yes; G
1757; Emerson; m; 17 (1915); F; s; son; yes; yes; G
1758; Lorenzo; m; 13 (1919); F; s; son; yes; yes; G
1759; Merrill; m; 3 (5-2-28); F; s; son; yes; yes; G

QUAVEHOMA

1760; Delbert; m; 27 (1905); F; m; Head; yes; yes; E
1761; (Polewenka), Renie; f; 25 (1907); F; m; wife; yes; yes; E
1762; Iola; f; 1 (8-5-30); F; s; dau; yes; yes; E

QUEHOYA

1763; Thornton; m; 26 (1906); F; m; Head; yes; yes; A
1764; Chloris; f; 22 (1910); F; m; wife; yes; yes; A

QUIMOYOUSI

1765; Dennis; m; 38 (1894); F; m; Head; yes; yes; I
1766; Berta; f; 32 (1900); F; m; wife; yes; yes; I
1767; Helen; f; 12 (1920); F; s; dau; yes; yes; I
1768; Herbert; m; 9 (1923); F; s; son; yes; yes; I
1769; Daniel; m; 6 (1926); F; s; son; yes; yes; I
1770; Max; m; 4 (11-20-27); F; s; son; yes; yes; I
1771; Dora; f; 1 (1931); F; s; dau; yes; yes; I

QUIO

1772; Jack; m; 53 (1879); F; s; Head; yes; yes; F

KEY: Census Number; Name; Sex; Age at Last Birthday; Tribe (Hopi, unless otherwise stated); Degree of Blood; Marital Status; Relationship to Head of Family; At Jurisdiction where enrolled [Yes or No] (If no, Where); Ward [Yes or No]; Hopi Village [according to key].

QUIQUA

1773; Martin; m; 33 (1899); F; m; Head; yes; yes; B
1774; Marietta; f; 31 (1901); F; m; wife; yes; yes; B
1775; Caroline; f; 9 (1923); F; s; dau; yes; yes; B
1776; Judson; m; 5 (5-27-26); F; s; son; yes; yes; B
1777; Herbert; m; 3 (4-11-28); F; s; son; yes; yes; B
1778; Margaret; f; 2 (1-23-30); F; s; dau; yes; yes; B

QUOMAHWAHU

1779; Nicholas; m; 34 (1898); F; m; Head; yes; yes; G
1780; Winnie; f; 30 (1902); F; m; wife; yes; yes; G
1781; Flora; f; 12 (1920); F; s; dau; yes; yes; G
1782; Pauline; f; 10 (1922); F; s; dau; yes; yes; G
1783; Marie; f; 7 (1925); F; s; dau; yes; yes; G
1784; Bertha Rose; f; 5 (3-1-27); F; s; dau; yes; yes; G
1785; Milton [Charles]; m; 3 (1929); F; s; son; yes; yes; G

QUOMANOMTIWA

1786; [Blank]; m; 71 (1861); F; m; Head; yes; yes; G
1787; Kelmoisi; f; 68 (1864); F; m; wife; yes; yes; G
1788; Susie; f; 16 (1916); F; s; dau; yes; yes; G

QUONESTEWA

1789; Steve; m; 60 (1872); F; m; Head; yes; yes; E
1790; Ahia; f; 55 (1877); F; m; wife; yes; yes; E
1791; **Beeson**, David; m; 29 (1903); F; s; son; yes; yes; E
1792; **Beeson**, Hugh; m; 22 (1910); F; s; son; yes; yes; E
1793; **Beeson**, Margaret; f; ?; F; s; dau; yes; yes; E
1794; **Beeson**, Elizabeth; f; 18 (1914); F; s; dau; yes; yes; E
1795; **Beeson**, Clarence; m; 16 (1916); F; s; son; yes; yes; E
1796; **Beeson**, Paul; m; 13 (1919); F; s; son; yes; yes; E

QUOTSHAYTIWA

1797; Roger; m; 55 (1877); f; m; Head; yes; yes; G
1798; Cecilia; f; 26 (1906); F; m; wife; yes; yes; G
1799; Joseph; m; 10 (1922); F; s; son; yes; yes; G
1800; Louis; m; 9 (1923); F; s; son; yes; yes; G
1801; Grace; f; 3 (1929); F; s; dau; yes; yes; G
1802; Julia Loretta; f; 4/12 (11-27-31); F; s; dau; yes; yes; G

HOPI INDIAN CENSUS, (As of April 1, 1932)

KEY: Census Number; Name; Sex; Age at Last Birthday; Tribe (Hopi, unless otherwise stated); Degree of Blood; Marital Status; Relationship to Head of Family; At Jurisdiction where enrolled [Yes or No] (If no, Where); Ward [Yes or No]; Hopi Village [according to key].

QUOTSKUYVA

1803; Willie; m; 43 (1889); F; m; Head; yes; yes; G
1804; Jennie; f; 43 (1889); F m; wife; yes; yes; G
1805; William; m; 24 (1908); F; s; son; yes; yes; G
1806; Bonnie; f; 22 (1910); F; s; dau; yes; yes; G
1807; Robert; m; 21 (1911); F; s; son; yes; yes; G
1808; Louise; f; 19 (1913); F; s; dau; yes; yes; G
1809; Ralph; m; 10 (1922); F; s; son; yes; yes; G
1810; Guy Edgar; m; 8 (1924); F; s; son; yes; yes; G
1811; Marietta; f; 6 (1926); F; s; dau; yes; yes; G
1812; Franklin; m; 4 (1928); F s; son; yes; yes; G
1813; Edwin; m; 3/12 (12-23-31); F; s; son; yes; yes; G

QUOYAWAYMA

1814; [Blank]; m; 59 (1873); F; m; Head; yes; yes; G
1815; Sivenqa; f; 67 (1865); F; m; wife; yes; yes; G
1816; Elizabeth; f; 39 (1893); F; s; dau; yes; yes; G
1817; Homer; m; 35 (1897); F; s; son; yes; yes; G
1818; Matthew; m; 31 (1901); F; s; son; yes; yes; G
1819; Alfred; m; 29 (1903); F; s; son; yes; yes; G
1820; Lydia; f; 24 (1908); F; s; dau; yes; yes; G

SACMUSSA

1821; [Blank]; m; 60 (1872); F; m; Head; yes; yes; D
1822; (Tawaninpka), [Blank]; f; 60 (1872); F; m; wife; yes; yes; D
1823; **Kayama**, Andy; m; 35 (1897); F; s; son; yes; yes; D
1824; **Naquayowma**, Ernest; m; 26 (1906); F; s; son; yes; yes; D
1825; **Masayowma,** Leonard; m; 19 (1913); F; s; son; yes; yes; D
1826; **Quayesi**, Will; m; 13 (1919); F; s; son; yes; yes; D

SACWYTEWA

1827; [Blank]; m; 55 (1877); F; m; Head; yes; yes; I
1828; Twaahbencie; f; 54 (1878); F; m; wife; yes; yes; I
1829; Harley; m; 20 (1912); F; s; nephew; yes; yes; I

SAHME

1830; [Blank]; m; 57 (1875); m; 57 (1875); F; m; Head; yes; yes; B
1831; Eva; f; 45 (1887); F; m; wife; yes; yes; B
1832; Foster; m; 17 (1915); F; s; son; yes; yes; B

70

KEY: Census Number; Name; Sex; Age at Last Birthday; Tribe (Hopi, unless otherwise stated); Degree of Blood; Marital Status; Relationship to Head of Family; At Jurisdiction where enrolled [Yes or No] (If no, Where); Ward [Yes or No]; Hopi Village [according to key].

1833; Eva Mae; f; 11 (1921); F; s; dau; yes; yes; B
1834; Donnelly; m; 9 (1923); F; s; son; yes; yes; B
1835; Clarice; f; 7 (1925); F; s; dau; yes; yes; B
1836; Lois; f; 3 (7-27-28); F; s; dau; yes; yes; B

SAHMEYAH

1837; Frank; m; 48 (1884); F; m; Head; yes; yes; C
1838; Lily; f; 46 (1886); F m; wife; yes; yes; C
1839; Ina; f; 22 (1910); F; s; dau; yes; yes; C
1840; Harold; m; 13 (1919); f; s; son; yes; yes; C
1841; Emily; f; 10 (1922); F; s; dau; yes; yes; C

SAHNAH

1842; [Blank]; m; 71 (1861); F; m; Head; yes; yes; C
1843; Yongah; f; 66 (1866); F; m; wife; yes; yes; C
1844; Hugh; m; 33 (1899); F; s; son; yes; yes; C

SAHNEYAH

1845; Sidney; m; 35 (1897); F; m; Head; yes; yes; A
1846; Ivy f; 37 (1895); F; m; wife; yes; yes; A
1847; Mabelle; f; 13 (1919); F; s; dau; yes; yes; A
1848; Harding; m; 11 (1921); F; s; son; yes; yes; A
1849; Paul S; m; 5 (10-8-26); F; s; son; yes; yes; A
1850; Hexman; m; 2 (5-12-29); F; s; son; yes; yes; A
1851; Russell; m; 9/12 (6-15-31); F; s; son; yes; yes; A
1852; **Dahlwepe**, Isabel; f; 19 (1913); F; s; ward; yes; yes; A
1853; **Dahlwepe**, Evelyn; f; 16 (1916); F; s; ward; yes; yes; A

SAKEWA

1854; Waldo; m; 33 (1899); F; m; Head; yes; yes; E
1855; (Coochinema), Violet; f; 27 (1905); F; m; wife; yes; yes; E
1856; Wallace; m; 8 (1924); F; s; son; yes; yes; E
1857; Nellie; f; 4 (9-12-27); F; s; dau; yes; yes; E
1858; Francis; m; 2 (6-26-29); F; s; son; yes; yes; E

SAKHONGOVA

1859; [Blank]; m; 52 (1880); F; m; Head; yes; yes; H
1860; Bessie; f; 51 (1881); F; m; wife; yes; yes; I

71

HOPI INDIAN CENSUS, (As of April 1, 1932)

KEY: Census Number; Name; Sex; Age at Last Birthday; Tribe (Hopi, unless otherwise stated); Degree of Blood; Marital Status; Relationship to Head of Family; At Jurisdiction where enrolled [Yes or No] (If no, Where); Ward [Yes or No]; Hopi Village [according to key].

SAKKOEYYOEMA

1861; [Blank]; m; 63 (1869); F; m; Head; yes; yes; I
1862; Gazrah; f; 55 (1877); F; m; wife; yes; yes; I

SAKMANEWA

1863; [Blank]; m; 55 (1877); F; w; Head; yes; yes; I

SAKWHONNIWA

1864; [Blank]; m; 50 (1882); F; m; Head; yes; yes; G
1865; Jane; f; 50 (1882); F; m; wife; yes; yes; G

SAKWONNOMTIWA

1866; [Blank]; m; 61 (1871); F; m; Head; yes; yes; G
1867; Kwanyawnom; f; 58 (1874); F; m; wife; yes; yes; G
1868; Hector; m; 33 (1899); F; s; son; yes; yes; G
1869; Matilda; f; 24 (1908); F; s; dau; yes; yes; G
1870; Lorenzo; m; 21 (1911); F; s; son; yes; yes; G
1871; Idella; f; 19 (1913); F; s; dau; yes; yes; G
1872; Lee; m; 16 (1916); F; s; yes; yes; G

SAKWYAMTIWA

1873; [Blank]; m; 63 (1869); F; w; Head; yes; yes; G

1874; Ellis; m; 24 (1908); F; m; Head; yes; yes; G
1875; Evalin; f; 23 (1909); F; m; wife; yes; yes; G

SANDERSON

1876; Georgiana; f; 25 (1907); F; m; wife; yes; yes; B
1877; Samuel O; m; 10 (1922); f; s; son; yes; yes; B
1878; Tom B: m; 9 (1923); F; s; son; yes; yes; B
1879; Edgar Miller; m; 4 (6-3-27); F; s; son; yes; yes; B
1880; Melvin Carl; m; 1 (1930); F; s; son; yes; yes; B

SATALA

1881; Baciese; m; 81 (1851); F; m; Head; yes; yes; C
1882; Saceumse; f; 64 (1868); F; m; wife; yes; yes; C
1883; Farris; m; 25 (1907); F; s; son; yes; yes; C

HOPI INDIAN CENSUS, (As of April 1, 1932)

KEY: Census Number; Name; Sex; Age at Last Birthday; Tribe (Hopi, unless otherwise stated); Degree of Blood; Marital Status; Relationship to Head of Family; At Jurisdiction where enrolled [Yes or No] (If no, Where); Ward [Yes or No]; Hopi Village [according to key].

1884; Robert; m; 34 (1898); F; m; Head; yes; yes; H
1885; Laura; f; 30 (1902); F; m; wife; yes; yes; H
1886; Edith; f; 8 (1924); F; s; dau; yes; yes; H
1887; Robert, Jr; m; 6 (1926); F; s; son; yes; yes; H
1888; Ruth; f; 3 (?-28-29); F; s; dau; yes; yes; H

SAYAHMA

1889; Walter; m; 38 (1894); F; m; Head; yes; yes; C
1890; Alberta; f; 26 (1906); F; m; wife; yes; yes; C
1891; Klaine; f; 4 (12-7-27); F; s; dau; yes; yes; C
1892; Hope; f; 3 (3-31-29); F; s; dau; yes; yes; C

SCHULACHIVIE

1893; Jason; m; 35 (1897); F; m; Head; yes; yes; B
1894; Gladys; f; 28 (1904); F; m; wife; yes; yes; B
1895; Otellie; f; 11 (1921); F; s; dau; yes; yes; B
1896; Jason, Jr; m; 8 (1924); F; s; son; yes; yes; B
1897; Eleedia; f; 3 (1929); F; s; dau; yes; yes; B
1898; Vann; m; 1 (12-20-30); F; s; son; yes; yes; B

SCOTT

1899; Seyouma [S.E.]; m; 33 (1899); F; w; Head; yes; yes; G
1900; Eddie; m; 10 (1922); F; s; son; yes; yes; G
1901; Ruby; f; 9 (1923); F; s; dau; yes; yes; G
1902; Warren; m; 7 ((1925); F; s; son; yes; yes; G
1903; Bryan; m; 5 (1927); F; s; son; yes; yes; G

SECATTALA

1904; [Blank]; m; 76 (1857); F; w; Head; yes; yes; B

SECAVEMA

1905; [Blank]; m; 65 (1867); F; m; Head; yes; yes; D
1906; (Salaco), [Blank]; f; 64 (1869); F; m; wife; yes; yes; D
1907; **Tawannimsie**, Sarah; f; 25 (1907); F; s; dau; yes; yes; D
1908; **Bavahonema**, Effie; f; 18 (1914); F; s; dau; yes; yes; D
1909; **Byestewa**, Conner; m; 15 (1917); F; s; son; yes; yes; D
1910; **Humeumptewa**, Vincent; m; 12 (1920); F; s; son; yes; yes; D
1911; **Kachina**, James; m; 45 (1887); F; w; bro-in-law; yes; yes; D
1912; **Kachina**, Lillian; f; 4 (1928); F; s; niece; yes; yes; D

73

KEY: Census Number; Name; Sex; Age at Last Birthday; Tribe (Hopi, unless otherwise stated); Degree of Blood; Marital Status; Relationship to Head of Family; At Jurisdiction where enrolled [Yes or No] (If no, Where); Ward [Yes or No]; Hopi Village [according to key].

SECLESTEWA

1913; [Blank]; m; 60 (1872); F; m; Head; yes; yes; D
1914; **Kashoinema**, Huldah; f; 35 (1897); F; m; wife; yes; yes; D
1915; **Kasheinema**, Eleanor; f; 14 (1918); F; s; dau; yes; yes; D
1916; **Kasheinema**, Wallace; m; 10 (1922); F; s; son; yes; yes; D
1917; **Kasheinema**, Helen; f; 8 (1924); F; s; dau; yes; yes; D
1918; **Kasheinema**, Frances; f; 2 (3-9-30); F; s; dau; yes; yes; D
1919; **Gilbert**, Bryan; m; 36 (1896); F; w; bro-in-law; yes; yes; D
1920; **Uyosie**, Lynn; m; 26 (1906; F; s; bro-in-law; yes; yes; D

SEECHA

1921; Homer; m; 22 (1910); F; m; Head; yes; yes; I
1922; Mabel; f; 23 (1909); F; m; wife; yes; yes; I
1923; Viola; f; 6/12 (9-13-31); F; s; dau; yes; yes; I

SEECHOMA

1924; Andrew; m; 33 (1899); F; m; Head; yes; yes; A
1925; Cora; f; 31 (1902); F; m; wife; yes; yes; A
1926; Joe; m; 11 (1921); F; s; son; yes; yes; A
1927; Willard; m; 8 (1924); F; s; son; yes; yes; A
1928; Robert Ed; m; 2 (11-15-29); F; s; son; yes; yes; A

SEEMAH

1929; Fritz; m; 52 (1880); F; m; Head; yes; yes; B
1930; Ella; f; 46 (1886); F; m; wife; yes; yes; B
1931; Guy; m; 17 (1915); F; s; son; yes; yes; B
1932; Amelia; f; 13 (1919); F; s; dau; yes; yes; B
1933; **Pooitema**, [Blank]; m; 64 (1868); F; w; uncle; yes; yes; B

SEENAHA

1934; Harry; m; 42 (1890); F; m; Head; yes; yes; I
1935; Grace; f; 40 (1892); F; m; wife; yes; yes; I
1936; Anna; f; 18 (1914); F; s; dau; yes; yes; I
1937; Alfred; m; 17 (1915); F; s; son; yes; yes; I

SEENI

1938; Herbert; m; 36 (1896); F; m; Head; yes; yes; B
1939; Kate; f; 35 (1897); F; m; wife; yes; yes; B

HOPI INDIAN CENSUS, (As of April 1, 1932)

KEY: Census Number; Name; Sex; Age at Last Birthday; Tribe (Hopi, unless otherwise stated); Degree of Blood; Marital Status; Relationship to Head of Family; At Jurisdiction where enrolled [Yes or No] (If no, Where); Ward [Yes or No]; Hopi Village [according to key].

1940; William; m; 19 (1913); F; s; son; yes; yes; B
1941; Blanche; f; 14 (1918); F; s; dau; yes; yes; B
1942; Dorothy; f; 10 (1922); F; s; dau; yes; yes; B
1943; Benson; m; 10/12 (6-23-31); F; s; son; yes; yes; B

SEEQUAPTEWA

1944; [Blank]; m; 54 (1878); F; m; Head; yes; yes; I
1945; Pahaquapnim; f; 49 (1883); F; m; wife; yes; yes; I
1946; Elmer; m; 20 (1912); F; s; son; yes; yes; I
1947; Fern; f; 18 (1914); F; s; dau; yes; yes; I
1948; Belle; f; 15 (1917); F; s; dau; yes; yes; I
1949; Loretta; f; 12 (1920); F; s; dau; yes; yes; I
1950; Edwin; m; 7 (1925); F; s; son; yes; yes; I
1951; Colton; m; 1/12 (2-2-32); F; s; son; yes; yes; I

SEEUKTEOMA

1952; Russell; m; 37 (1895); F; m; Head; yes; yes; H
1953; Ethel; f; 36 (1896); F; m; wife; yes; yes; H
1954; Hildah; f; 15 (1917); F; s; dau; yes; yes; H
1955; Leo; m; 8 (1924); F; s; son; yes; yes; H
1956; David; m; 6 (1926); F; s; son; yes; yes; H
1957; Iris; f; 4 (6-2-27); F; s; dau; yes; yes; H
1958; Clyde; m; 1 (1931); F; s; son; yes; yes; H

SEEZRO

1959; Claude; m; 29 (1903); F; m; Head; yes; yes; F
1960; Fay; f; 20 (1902); F; m; wife; yes; yes; F
1961; Leroy; m; 9 (1923); F; s; son; yes; yes; F
1962; Eldon; m; 1 (10-6-30); F; s; son; yes; yes; F

SEHEPTEWA

1963; [Blank]; m; 65 (1867); F; m; Head; yes; yes; I
1964; (Sehepnim), [Blank]; f; 59 (1873); F; m; wife; yes; yes; I
1965; **Talanimptewa**, [Blank]; m; 67 (1865); F; s; bro; yes; yes; I

SEHONGVA

1966; [Blank]; m; 68 (1864); F; m; Head; yes; yes; I
1967; Masahongka; f; 59 (1873); F; m; wife; yes; yes; I
1968; Janet; f; 21 (1911); F; s; dau; yes; yes; I

HOPI INDIAN CENSUS, (As of April 1, 1932)

KEY: Census Number; Name; Sex; Age at Last Birthday; Tribe (Hopi, unless otherwise stated); Degree of Blood; Marital Status; Relationship to Head of Family; At Jurisdiction where enrolled [Yes or No] (If no, Where); Ward [Yes or No]; Hopi Village [according to key].

SEHONGSE

1969; Perry; m; 24 (1908); F; m; Head; yes; yes; H
1970; Rose; f; 24 (1908); F; m; wife; yes; yes; H

SEIMATEWA

1971; Howard; m; 34 (1898); F; m; Head; yes; yes; A
1972; Viola; f; 33 (1899); F; m; wife; yes; yes; A
1973; Calvin; m; 2 (1930); F; s; son; yes; yes; A
1974; Violet Ethel; f; 2/12 (1-5-32); F; s; dau; yes; yes; A

SEQUAPTEWA

1975; Emory; m; 37 (1895); F; m; Head; yes; yes; I
1976; Helen; f; 31 (1901); F; m; wife; yes; yes; I
1977; Wayne; m; 8 (1924); F; s; son; yes; yes; I
1978; Eugene; m; 6 (1926); F; s; son; yes; yes; I
1979; Emory, Jr; m; 4 (12-29-27); F; s; son; yes; yes; I
1980; Abbott; m; 2 (12-4-29); F; s; son; yes; yes; I
1981; **Talashonewa**, Sam; m; 69 (1863); F; w; father-in-law; yes; yes; I
1982; **Lomakaka**, Lawrence; m; 19 (1913); F; s; bro-in-law; yes; yes; I

SEKATAYOU

1983; Roy; m; 32 (1900); F; w; Head; yes; yes; D
1984; Willard; m; 10 (192); F; s; son; yes; yes; D
1985; Ida Lee; f; 9 (1923); F; s; dau; yes; yes; D
1986; Elvan; m; 4 (1928); F; s; son; yes; yes; D

SEKAWYMA

1987; Albert; m; 35 (1897); F; m; Head; yes; yes; A
1988; Emma; f; 26 (1906); F; m; wife; yes; yes; A

1989; Lena; f; 44 (1888); F; w; Head; yes; yes; A
1990; Mary L; f; 11 (1921); F; s; dau; yes; yes; A
1991; **Chio**, Sunbeam; f; 19 (1913); f; s; dau; yes;yes; A
1992; **Chio**, Forest; m; 17 (1915); F; s; son; yes; yes; A
1993; **Chio**, Alfreda; f; 4 (1929); F; s; dau; yes; yes; A

SEKAYIMPTEWA

1994; Aquilla; m; 37 (1895; F; m; Head; yes; yes; I

76

KEY: Census Number; Name; Sex; Age at Last Birthday; Tribe (Hopi, unless otherwise stated); Degree of Blood; Marital Status; Relationship to Head of Family; At Jurisdiction where enrolled [Yes or No] (If no, Where); Ward [Yes or No]; Hopi Village [according to key].

1995; Sadie; f; 39 (1893); F; m; wife; yes; yes; I
1996; Wallie; m; 16 (1916); F; s; son; yes; yes; I
1997; Allie; f; 14 (1918); F; s; dau; yes; yes; I
1998; Dayton; m; 6 (1926); F; s; son; yes; yes; I
1999; Roberta; f; 5 (2-25-27); F; s; dau; yes; yes; I

SEKAYOMA

2000; Jack; m; 53 (1879); F; m; Head; yes; yes; F
2001; Wilhimina; f; 41 (1891); F; m; wife; yes; yes; F
2002; Bessie; f; 19 (1913); F; s; dau; yes; yes; F
2003; Earl; f; 17 (1915); F; s; son; yes; yes; F
2004; **Nevayumptewa**, Fred; m; 32 (1900); F; s; nephew; yes; yes; F

SEKAYUMPTEWA

2005; Charles; m; 69 (1863); F; w; Head; yes; yes; F
2006; Elmer; m; 39 (1893); F; s; son; yes; yes; F
2007; Emaline; f; 20 (1912); F; s; dau; yes; yes; F

SEKESTEWA

2008; Robert; m; ?; F; m; Head; yes; yes; [village not given]
2009; (Ahealing), Beatrice; f; 20 (1912); F; m; wife; yes; yes; [village not given]

SEKIYOWMA

2010; Frank; m; 43 (1889); F; m; Head; yes; yes; I
2011; Phoeba; f; 40 (1892); F; m; wife; yes; yes; I
2012; Moses; m; 20 (1912); F; s; son; yes; yes; I
2013; Isaac; m; 19 (1914); F; s; son; yes; yes; I
2014; Victoria; f; 16 (1916); F; s; dau; yes; yes; I
2015; Marcus; m; 13 (1919); F; s; son; yes; yes; I
2016; Jacob; m; 11 (1921); F; s; son; yes; yes; I
2017; Luella; f; 8 (1924); F; s; dau; yes; yes; I
2018; Ethel; f; 2 (11-11-29); F; s; dau; yes; yes; I

SIMATZKUKU

2019; [Blank]; m; 51 (1881); F; m; Head; yes; yes; I
2020; Choseyownim; f; 49 (1883); F; m; wife; no; Western Navajo, P.O. Tuba City, Coconino Co, AZ; yes; I
2021; Dewan; m; 29 (1903); F; s; son; no; Insane asylum; P.O. Phoenix, Maricopa Co, AZ; yes; I

77

HOPI INDIAN CENSUS, (As of April 1, 1932)

KEY: Census Number; Name; Sex; Age at Last Birthday; Tribe (Hopi, unless otherwise stated); Degree of Blood; Marital Status; Relationship to Head of Family; At Jurisdiction where enrolled [Yes or No] (If no, Where); Ward [Yes or No]; Hopi Village [according to key].

2022; Fenton; m; 17 (1915); F; s; son; no; Indian School, P.O. Phoenix, Maricopa Co, AZ; yes; I

2023; Edward; m; 13 (1919); F; s; son; no; Sherman Institute, P.O. Riverside, [Blank] Co, CA; yes; I

2024; Norman; m; 8 (?); F; s; son; no; Western Navajo, P.O. Tuba City, Coconino Co, AZ; yes; I

SEMEHOVA

2025; Clark; m; 26 (1906); F; m; Head; yes; yes; E

2026; (Poleynema), Joyce; f; 18 (1914); F; m; wife; yes; yes; E

SEQUEVA

2027; [Blank]; m; 59 (1873); F; m; Head; yes; yes; E

2028; (Koyawynema), [Blank]; f; 58 (1874); F; m; wife; yes; yes; E

SEQUI

2029; [Blank]; m; 44 (1888); F; m; Head; yes; yes; A

2030; Edna; f; 39 (1893); F; m; wife; yes; yes; A

2031; **Lahpoo**, Aubrey; m; 21 (1911); F; s; son; yes; yes; A

2032; Hugh; m; 14 (1918); F; s; son; yes; yes; A

2033; Ellen; f; 9 (19230; F; s; dau; yes; yes; A

2034; Melvina; f; 5 (4-5-26); F; s; dau; yes; yes; A

2035; Vera; f; 3 (8-2-28); F; s; dau; yes; yes; A

2036; Everett; m; 1 (11-18-30); F; s; son; yes; yes; A

SETIMA

2037; [Blank]; m; 64 (1868); F; m; Head; yes; yes; B

2038; Dakevanka; f; 60 (1872); F; m; wife; yes; yes; B

2039; Ben; m; 31 (1901); F; m; Head; yes; yes; D

2040; Anna Mae; f; 28 (1904); F; m; wife; yes; yes; D

2041; Elsa Neva; f; 5 (1927); F; s; dau; yes; yes; D

2042; Alphfrieda; f; 2 (1930); F; s; dau; yes; yes; D

SEWEUMPTEWA

2043; Moses; m; 46 (1886); F; m; Head; yes; yes; D

2044; (Joswenka), Barbara; f; 31 (1901); F; m; wife; yes; yes; D

2045; Dean; m; 10 (1922); F; s; son; yes; yes; D

2046; Lavern; m; 7 (1925); F; s; son; yes; yes; D

2047; Velma; f; 4 (3-23-28); F; s; dau; yes; yes; D

KEY: Census Number; Name; Sex; Age at Last Birthday; Tribe (Hopi, unless otherwise stated); Degree of Blood; Marital Status; Relationship to Head of Family; At Jurisdiction where enrolled [Yes or No] (If no, Where); Ward [Yes or No]; Hopi Village [according to key].

2048; Eldon; m; 7/12 (9-12-31); F; s; son; yes; yes; D

SEYESTEWA

2049; [Blank]; m; 50 (1882); F; m; Head; yes; yes; D
2050; (Coochownema), [Blank]; f; 48 (1884); F; m; wife; yes; yes; D

SEYOWMA

2051; [Blank]; m; 60 (1872); F; m; Head; yes; yes; G
2052; Tuvehumana; f; 58 (1874); F; m; wife; yes; yes; G
2053; Ralph; m; 34 (1898); F; s; son; yes; yes; G
2054; Lois; f; 25 (1907); F; s; dau; yes; yes; G
2055; Alfred m; 23 (1909); F; s; son; yes; yes; G
2056; Frieda; f; 19 (1913); F; s; adpt-dau; yes; yes; G

SHAYOYA

2057; Ray; m; 53 (1879); F; m; Head; yes; yes; H
2058; Schongee; f; 60 (1872); F; m; wife; yes; yes; H
2059; Ellen; f; 27 (1905); F; s; dau; yes; yes; H
2060; Alonzo; m; 19 (1913); F; s; son; yes; yes; H
2061; Jessie; f; 14 (1918); F; s; stp-dau; yes; yes; H
2062; Raymond; m; 12 (1920); F; s; stp-son; yes; yes; H

SHELTON

2063; Peter; m; 26 (1906); F; m; Head; yes; yes; G
2064; Lily; f; 25 (1907); F; m; wife; yes; yes; G
2065; Peter, Jr; m; 4 (6-4-27); F; s; son; yes; yes; G
2066; Henry; m; 3 (2-1-29); F; s; son; yes; yes; G
2067; Betsy; f; 1 (3-20-31); F; s; dau; yes; yes; G

SHUNKEE

2068; Hale; m; 43 (1889); F; m; Head; yes; yes; B
2069; Emma; f; 38 (1894); F; m; wife; yes; yes; B
2070; Pansy; f; 20 (1912); F; s; dau; yes; yes; B
2071; Marcella; f; 16 (1916); F; s; dau; yes; yes; B
2072; Marty; m; 11 (1921); F; s; son; yes; yes; B
2073; Burke; m; 8 (1924); F; s; son; yes; yes; B
2074; Ramona; f; 3 (2-16-29); F; s; dau; yes; yes; B
2075; Ward; m; 3/12 (1-1-32); F; s; son; yes; yes; B

HOPI INDIAN CENSUS, (As of April 1, 1932)

KEY: Census Number; Name; Sex; Age at Last Birthday; Tribe (Hopi, unless otherwise stated); Degree of Blood; Marital Status; Relationship to Head of Family; At Jurisdiction where enrolled [Yes or No] (If no, Where); Ward [Yes or No]; Hopi Village [according to key].

SHUPULA

2076; Mary; f; 50 (1882); F; w; Head; yes; yes; A
2077; Alex Roger; m; 21 (1911); F; s; son; yes; yes; A
2078; Jerome; m; 18 (1914); F; s; son; yes; yes; A
2079; Franklin; m; 9 (1923); F; s; son; yes; yes; A

2080; Edgar; m; 43 (1889); F; m; Head; yes; yes; A
2081; Hazel; f; 30 (1902); F; m; wife; yes; yes; A
2082; Beth; f; 4 (12-4-87); F; s; dau; yes; yes; A
2083; Leonard; m; 2 (11-17-29); F; s; son; yes; yes; A
2084; Douglas; m; 6/12 (9-21-31); F; s; son; yes; yes; A

SIHEVEIMA

2085; Arthur; m; 42 (1890); F; m; Head; yes; yes; G
2086; Pearl; f; 48 (1884); F; m; wife; yes; yes; G

2087; Barbara; f; 32 (1900); F; w; Head; yes; yes; G
2088; Paul; m; 20 (1912); F; s; son; yes; yes; G
2089; Marjorie; f; 16 (1916); F; s; dau; yes; yes; G
2090; Norman; m; 7 (1925); F; s; son; yes; yes; G
2091; Madge; f; 5 (10-5-27); F; s; dau; yes; yes; G
2092; Frank; m; 1 (12-16-30); F; s; son; yes; yes; G

SIKONQA

2093; Rachel; f; 23 (1909); F; s; Head; yes; yes; G

SIKAHEINEMA

2094; [Blank]; f; 61 (1871); F; w; Head; yes; yes; G

SIKAYISTIWA

2095; Howard; m; 34 (1898); F; m; Head; yes; yes; G
2096; Jessie; f; 23 (1899); F; m; wife; yes; yes; G
2097; Marian; f; 12 (1920); F; s; dau; yes; yes; G
2098; Elizabeth; f; 9 (1923); F; s; dau; yes; yes; G

2099; Joe; m; 65 (1867); F; m; Head; yes; yes; G
2100; Allie; f; 63 (1869); F; m; wife; yes; yes; G
2101; Robert; m; 33 (1899); F; s; son; yes; yes; G
2102; Willard; m; 27 (1905); F; s; son; yes; yes; G

HOPI INDIAN CENSUS, (As of April 1, 1932)

KEY: Census Number; Name; Sex; Age at Last Birthday; Tribe (Hopi, unless otherwise stated); Degree of Blood; Marital Status; Relationship to Head of Family; At Jurisdiction where enrolled [Yes or No] (If no, Where); Ward [Yes or No]; Hopi Village [according to key].

2103; Lyndal; m; 19 (1913); F; s; son; yes; yes; G
2104; Abbott; m; 16 (1916); F; s; son; yes; yes; G
2105; Elma; f; 26 (1906); F; s; adpt-dau; yes; yes; G

2106; Victor; m; 37 (1895); F; m; Head; yes; yes; G
2107; Ramona; f; 32 (1900); F; m; wife; yes; yes; G
2108; Victor, Jr; m; 12 (1920); F; s; son; yes; yes; G
2109; Manuel; m; 11 (1921); F; s; son; yes; yes; G

SILAS

2110; Stephen; m; 32 (1900); F; m; Head; yes; yes; B
2111; Evelyn; f; 30 (1902); F; m; wife; yes; yes; B
2112; Mae; f; 10 (1922); F; s; dau; yes; yes; B
2113; Pauline; f; 4 (6-21-27); F; s; dau; yes; yes; B
2114; Anna; f; 3/12 (12-5-31); F; s; son; yes; yes; B

2115; Tom A; m; 37 (1895); F; m; Head; yes; yes; B
2116; Annette; f; 26 (1906); F; m; wife; yes; yes; B
2117; Matthew; m; 10 (1922); F; s; son; yes; yes; B
2118; Emma; f; 7 (1925); F; s; dau; yes; yes; B
2119; Gertrude; f; 4 (12-13-27); F; s; dau; yes; yes; B
2120; Judith; f; 1 (?); F; s; dau; yes; yes; B

SINGYOWMA

2121; [Blank]; m; 53(1879); F; m; Head; yes; yes; D
2122; (Kachmanna), Cora; f; 32 (1900); F; m; wife; yes; yes; D
2123; **Lomachutskeoma**, Elmo; m; 19 (1913); F; s; son; yes; yes; D
2124; **Kaoyesnema**, Hallie; f; 18 (1914); F; s; dau; yes; yes; D
2125; **Masiyesnema**, Maud; f; 13 (1919); F; s; dau; yes; yes; D

SINOITIWA

2126; [Blank]; m; 68 (1864); F; w; Head; yes; yes; G

SINOIVA

2127; [Blank]; m; 63 (1869); F; w; Head; yes; yes; G

SOEQUESVA

2128; Burton; m; 34 (1898); F; m; Head; yes; yes; H
2129; Maud; f; 28 (1904); F; m; wife; yes; yes; H

81

KEY: Census Number; Name; Sex; Age at Last Birthday; Tribe (Hopi, unless otherwise stated); Degree of Blood; Marital Status; Relationship to Head of Family; At Jurisdiction where enrolled [Yes or No] (If no, Where); Ward [Yes or No]; Hopi Village [according to key].

2130; Marion; f; 10 (1922); F; s; dau; yes; yes; H
2131; Ione; f; 8 (1924); F; s; dau; yes; yes; H
2132; Evert; m; 2 (12-5-29); F; s; son; yes; yes; H
2133; Jessie; f; 2/12 (1-20-32); F; s; dau; yes; yes; H

SOSNEWA

2134; Raymond; m; 32 (1900); F; m; Head; yes; yes; E
2135; (Yoevenise), Alta; f; 27 (1905); F; m; wife; yes; yes; E
2136; Susie Charlotte; f; 4 (6-16-27); F; s; dau; yes; yes; E
2137; Howard; m; 2 (6-11-29); F; s; son; yes; yes; E
2138; **Kachawwaicha**, Bertha; f; 5 (6-11-26); F; s; dau; yes; yes; E
2139; Nita; f; 4/12 (11-11-31); F; s; dau; yes; yes; E

SOUFKIMA

2140; Paul; m; 27 (1905); F; w; Head; yes; yes; F
2141; May; f; 7 (1925); F; s; dau; yes; yes; F

SUETOPKA

2142; Edward; m; 44 (1888); F; m; Head; yes; yes; I
2143; Florence; f; 42 (1890); F; m; wife; yes; yes; I
2144; Emma; f; 19 (1913); F; s; dau; yes; yes; I
2145; Willie; m; 15 (1917); F; s; son; yes; yes; I
2146; Guy; m; 13 (1919); F; s; son; yes; yes; I
2147; Neilson; m; 10 (1922); F; s; son; yes; yes; I
2148; Vinton; m; 7 (1925); F; s; son; yes; yes; I
2149; Edward; m; 4 (7-9-27); F; s; son; yes; yes; I
2150; Evelyn; f; 1 (1930); F; s; dau; yes; yes; I

SULU

2151; [Blank]; m; 68 (1864); F; m; Head; yes; yes; A
2152; Pootsa; f; 58 (1874); F; m; wife; yes; yes; A
2153; Timothy; m; 25 (1907); F; s; son; yes; yes; A
2154; Joan; f; 20 (1912); F; s; dau; yes; yes; A

SUSUMKEWA

2155; [Blank]; m; 60 (1872); F; w; Head; yes; yes; D
2156; Talitha; f; 18 (1914); F; s; dau; yes; yes; D
2157; Wayne; m; 17 (1915); F; s; son; yes; yes; D
2158; Neilson; m; 15 (1917); F; s; son; yes; yes; D

HOPI INDIAN CENSUS, (As of April 1, 1932)

KEY: Census Number; Name; Sex; Age at Last Birthday; Tribe (Hopi, unless otherwise stated); Degree of Blood; Marital Status; Relationship to Head of Family; At Jurisdiction where enrolled [Yes or No] (If no, Where); Ward [Yes or No]; Hopi Village [according to key].

2159; Emerson; m; 14 (1918); F; s; son; yes; yes; D
2160; Althea; f; 10 (1922); f; s; dau; yes; yes; D

SUTTAH

2161; Allison; m; 21 (1911); F; s; Head; yes; yes; B
2162; Wadsworth; m; 15 (1917); F; s; son; yes; yes; B

SUTYEMA

2163; George; m; 39 (1893); F; m; Head; yes; yes; I
2164; May; f; 37 (1895); F; m; wife; yes; yes; I
2165; Paul; m; 17 (1915); F; s; son; yes; yes; I

SUYESCIA

2166; Forest; m; 43 (1889); F; s; Head; yes; yes; E

TAHBO

2167; Taylor; m; 44 (1888); F; w; Head; yes; yes; A
2168; Olson; m; 17 (1915); F; s; son; yes; yes; A
2169; Naomi; f; 10 (1922); F; s; dau; yes; yes; A
2170; Taylor, Jr; m; 8 (1924); F; s; son; yes; yes; A
2171; Lorenzo; m; 6 (2-19-26); F; s; son; yes; yes; A

TAHIAHWINNUH

2172; Silas Hopi; m; 50 (1882); F; s; Head; yes; yes; C

TAHLETSTEMAH

2173; Barney; m; 25 (1907); F; m; Head; yes; yes; C
*2172; Nora; f; 3 (5-16-28); ½; s; dau; yes; yes; C

[*NOTE: Number given twice]

TAHO

2173; **Tuveyamtiwa**, Leonard; m; 44 (1888); F; w; Head; yes; yes; G
2174; Wilbert; m; 1 (6-26-30); F; s; son; yes; yes; G

KEY: Census Number; Name; Sex; Age at Last Birthday; Tribe (Hopi, unless otherwise stated); Degree of Blood; Marital Status; Relationship to Head of Family; At Jurisdiction where enrolled [Yes or No] (If no, Where); Ward [Yes or No]; Hopi Village [according to key].

TALAHAFTEWA

2175; Clarke; m; 57 (1895); F; m; Head; yes; yes; F
2176; Lucy; f; 40 (1892); F; m; wife; yes; yes; F
2177; James; m; 20 (1912); F; s; son; yes; yes; F
2178; William; m; 9 (1925); F; s; grnd-son yes; yes; F

2179; Herbert; m; 23 (1909); F; m; Head; yes; yes; F
2180; Evangeline; f; 20 (1912); F; m; wife; yes; yes; F
2181; Lena; f; 10/12 (6-12-32); F; s; dau; yes; yes; F

TALAS

2182; Homer; m; 35 (1897); F; m; Head; yes; yes; G
2183; Sylvia; f; 28 (1904); F; m; wife; yes; yes; G
2184; Blanch; f; 8 (1924); F; s; dau; yes; yes; G
2185; Pearl; f; 6 (3-22-26); F; s; dau; yes; yes; G
2186; Donald; m; 3 (9-8-28); F; s; son; yes; yes; G

TALASHOEMA

2187; Webster; m; 36 (1896); F; m; Head; yes; yes; H
2188; Abby; f; 35 (1897); F; m; wife; yes; yes; H
2189; Wilbur; m; 8 (1924); F; s; son; yes; yes; H
2190; Ada; f; 14 (1918); F; s; dau; yes; yes; H

2191; [Blank]; m; 63 (1869); F; m; Head; yes; yes; H
2192; Sakhonghim; f; 61 (1871); F; m; wife; yes; yes; H
2193; Barbara; f; 27 (1905); F; s; dau; yes; yes; H
2194; Wilson; m; 25 (1907); F; s; son; yes; yes; H
2195; Naomi; f; 18 (1914); F; s; dau; yes; yes; H
2196; **Poleyyma**, Idella; f; 16 (1916); F; s; grnd-dau; yes; yes; H
2197; **Poleyyma**, Dorothy; f; 12 (1920); F; s; grnd-dau; yes; yes; H
2198; **Poleyyma**, Walter; m; 9 (1923); F; s; grnd-son; yes; yes; H

TALASHOYNIWA

2199; [Blank]; m; 78 (1854); F; w; Head; yes; yes; G

TALASKWAPTIWA

2200; Bert; m; 58 (1874); F; s; Head; yes; yes; G

HOPI INDIAN CENSUS, (As of April 1, 1932)

KEY: Census Number; Name; Sex; Age at Last Birthday; Tribe (Hopi, unless otherwise stated); Degree of Blood; Marital Status; Relationship to Head of Family; At Jurisdiction where enrolled [Yes or No] (If no, Where); Ward [Yes or No]; Hopi Village [according to key].

TALASNOMTIWA

2201; [Blank]; f; 63 (1869); F; w; Head; yes; yes; G
2202; Amy; f; 31 (1901); F; s; dau; yes; yes; G

TALASSHO

2203; [Blank]; m; 55(1877); F; m; Head; yes; yes; C
2204; Lomaho; f; 53 (1879); F; m; wife; yes; yes; C
2205; Laura; f; 21 (1911); F; s; dau; yes; yes; C
2206; May; f; 11 (1921); F; s; dau; yes; yes; C

2207; Ole; m; 32 (1900); F; m; Head; yes; yes; C
2208; (Tahbo), Adela; f; 14 (2-22-18); F; m; wife; yes; yes; C

TALASVEIMA

2209; [Blank]; m; 69 (1864); F; m; Head; yes; yes; G
2210; Ila; f; 60 (1872); F; m; wife; yes; yes; G
2211; Helen; f; 18 (1914); F; s; dau; yes; yes; G

TALASWAHUMA

2212; Judge; m; 61 (1871); F; w; Head; yes; yes; D
2213; **Chong**, John; m; 15 (1917); F; s; son; yes; yes; D
2214; Della; f; 10 (1922); F; s; dau; yes; yes; D

TALASWINTEWA

2215; [Blank]; m; 55 (1877); F; s; Head; yes; yes; F

TALASWOEMA

2216; [Blank]; m; 88 (1844); F; w; Head; yes; yes; H

TALASWYTEWA

2217; [Blank]; m; 65 (1869); F; m; Head; yes; yes; H
2218; Tewanimsie; f; 64 (1868); F; m; wife; yes; yes; H
2219; Marsa; f; 22 (1910); F; s; dau; yes; yes; H
2220; Taylor; m; 19 (1913); F; s; son; yes; yes; H
2221; Clara; f; 24 (1908); F; s; dau; yes; yes; H
2222; John; m; 29 (1903); F; s; son; yes; yes; H

85

KEY: Census Number; Name; Sex; Age at Last Birthday; Tribe (Hopi, unless otherwise stated); Degree of Blood; Marital Status; Relationship to Head of Family; At Jurisdiction where enrolled [Yes or No] (If no, Where); Ward [Yes or No]; Hopi Village [according to key].

TALASYOSEA

2223; [Blank]; m; 44 (1888); F; m; Head; yes; yes; D
2224; (Polewuh), Amelia; f; 44 (1888); F; m; wife; yes; yes; D
2225; **Masayowma**, Lola; f; 25 (1907); F; s; dau; yes; yes; D
2226; **Quamasie**, Estella; f; 16 (1916); F; s; dau; yes; yes; D
2227; Pauline; f; 3 (4-5-28); F; s; dau; yes; yes; D
2228; Latha; f; 10/12 (5-3-21); F; s; dau; yes; yes; D
2229; **Hermeletstewa**, [Blank]; m; 65 (1867); F; w; father-in-law; yes; yes; D

TALAUMPTEWA

2230; Jack; m; 47 (1885); F; m; Head; yes; yes; A
2231; Lydia; f; 32 (1900); F; m; wife; yes; yes; A
2232; Mark; f; 25 (1907); F; s; son; yes; yes; A
2233; Vernon; m; 19 (1913); F; s; son; yes; yes; A
2234; Sybil; f; 16 (1916); F; s; dau; yes; yes; A
2235; Henry; m; 11 (1921); F; s; son; yes; yes; A
2236; Jack, Jr; m; 9 (1923); F; s; son; yes; yes; A
2237; Lettie; f; 6 (1926); F; s; dau yes; yes; A
2238; Stella; f; 2 (9-23-29); F; s; dau; yes; yes; A

TALAWAYTIWA

2239; Alban; m; 25 (1907); F; s; Head; yes; yes; G
2240; Ernest; m; 19 (1913); F; s; bro; yes; yes; G
2241; Imogene; f; 18 (1914); F; s; sis; yes; yes; G
2242; Joel; m; 16 (1916); F; s; bro; yes; yes; G

TALAWIFTEWA

2243; David; m; 42 (1890); F; m; Head; yes; yes; E
2244; (Honumpka), Alice; f; 42 (1890); F; m; wife; yes; yes; E
2245; **Zalawr**, Grant; m; 37 (1895); F; s; bro-in-law; yes; yes; E

*TALAWISTMA or TALAWISUMA

2246; Rachel; f; 68 (1864); F; w; Head; yes; yes; F

[**NOTE:** Difficult to read name, type smeared]

TALAWISUMA

2247; Ralph; m; 29 (1903); F; m; Head; yes; yes; F

KEY: Census Number; Name; Sex; Age at Last Birthday; Tribe (Hopi, unless otherwise stated); Degree of Blood; Marital Status; Relationship to Head of Family; At Jurisdiction where enrolled [Yes or No] (If no, Where); Ward [Yes or No]; Hopi Village [according to key].

2248; Chloe; f; 28 (19040; F; m; wife; yes; yes; F
2249; Vincent; m; 2 (9-1-29); F; s; son; yes; yes; F
2250; Annabel; f; 1 (3-10-31); F; s; dau; yes; yes; F

TALAYUMPTEWA

2251; Howard; m; 37 (1895); F; m; Head; yes; yes; H
2252; Mabel; f; 37 (1895); F; m; wife; yes; yes; H
2253; Norris; m; 17 (1915); F; s; son; yes; yes; H
2254; Orville; m; 10 (1922); F; s; son; yes; yes; H
2255; Martin; m; 6 (3-17-26); F; s; son; yes; yes; H
2256; Esther; f; 1 (1930); F; s; dau; yes; yes; H

2257; Washington; m; 43 (1889); F; m; Head; yes; yes; F
2258; May; f; 43 (1889); F; m; wife; yes; yes; F
2259; Willis; m; 17 (1915); F; s; son; yes; yes; F
2260; Carl; m; 9 (1923); F; s; son; yes; yes; F
2261; Mawa; m; 5 (4-12-26); F; s; son; yes; yes; F
2262; Tressa; f; 9 (1923); F; s; grnd-dau; yes; yes; F
2263; Nova; f; 3 (1929); F; s; grnd-dau; yes; yes; F

TAKALA

2264; Thomas; m; 40 (1892); F; m; Head; yes; yes; I
2265; Ruth; f; 46 (1886); F; m; wife; yes; yes; I
2266; Agnes; f; 20 (1912); F; s; dau; yes; yes; I
2267; Edith; f; 17 (1915); F; s; dau; yes; yes; I
2268; Dewey; m; 10 (1922); F; s; son; yes; yes; I
2269; Don Miles; m; 6 (1926); F; s; son; yes; yes; I
2270; Owen; m; 10/12 (5-21-31); F; s; son; yes; yes; I

2271; Roscoe; m; 57 (1875); F; m; Head; yes; yes; B
2272; Ruth; f; 55 (1877); F; m; wife; yes; yes; B
2273; Bertha; f; 27 (1905); F; s; dau; yes; yes; B
2274; Julia; f; 19 (1913); F; s; dau; yes; yes; B
2275; Paul A; m; 10 (1922); F; s; son; yes; yes; B
2276; Loretta; f; 8 (1924); f; s; dau; yes; yes; B

TANAKEYOWMA

2277; [Blank]; m; 48 (1884); F; m; Head; yes; yes; I
2278; Ceynom; f; 50 (1882); F; m; wife; yes; yes; I
2279; Patrick; m; 21 (1911); F; s; son; yes; yes; I
2280; Clyde; m; 19 (1913); F; s; son; yes; yes; I

KEY: Census Number; Name; Sex; Age at Last Birthday; Tribe (Hopi, unless otherwise stated); Degree of Blood; Marital Status; Relationship to Head of Family; At Jurisdiction where enrolled [Yes or No] (If no, Where); Ward [Yes or No]; Hopi Village [according to key].

2281; Etta; f; 15 (1817); F; s; dau; yes; yes; I
2282; Zetta; f; 12 (1920); F; s; dau; yes; yes; I
2283; Jason; m; 8 (1924); F; s; son; yes; yes; I

TAWAHIEOMA

2284; Starlie; m; 30 (1902); F; m; Head; yes; yes; D
2285; (Tawakyonem), [Blank]; f; 27 (1905); F; m; wife; yes; yes; D
2286; Anita; f; 9 (1923); F; s; dau; yes; yes; D
2287; Starlie, Jr; m; 7 (1925); F; s; son; yes; yes; D
2288; Williams; m; 5 (1927); F; s; son; yes; yes; D
2289; Nancy; f; 2 (6-18-29); F; s; dau; yes; yes; D
2290; Garland; m; 2 (5-8-31); F; s; son; yes; yes; D

TAWAHONGEOMA

2291; William; m; 28 (1904); F; m; Head; yes; yes; H

2292; [Blank]; m; 64 (1868); F; m; Head; yes; yes; H
2293; Mayee; f; 63 (1869); F; m; wife; yes; yes; H
2294; Wallace; m; 21 (1911); F; s; son; yes; yes; H
2295; Lucas; m; 18 (1914); F; s; son; yes; yes; H

2296; [Blank]; m; 63 (1869); F; m; Head; yes; yes; I
2297; Koyomgnoka; f; 59 (1873); F; m; wife; yes; yes; I
2298; Chester; m; 17 (1915); F; s; son; yes; yes; I
2299; Sarah; f; 13 (1919); F; s; dau; yes; yes; I
2300; Della; f; 9 (1923); F; s; dau; yes; yes; I

TAWAHONQA

2301; Tillie; f; 35 (1897); F; s; Head; yes; yes; G

TAWAKWAPTIWA

2302; Wilson; m; 59 (1873); F; m; Head; yes; yes; G
2303; Lizzie; f; 59 (1873); F; m; wife; yes; yes; G

TAWALETSTEWA

2304; Rudolph; m; 59 (1873); F; w; Head; yes; yes; D

KEY: Census Number; Name; Sex; Age at Last Birthday; Tribe (Hopi, unless otherwise stated); Degree of Blood; Marital Status; Relationship to Head of Family; At Jurisdiction where enrolled [Yes or No] (If no, Where); Ward [Yes or No]; Hopi Village [according to key].

TAWAMAYHIM

2305; [Blank]; m; 99 (1833); F; w; Head; yes; yes; E

TAWANGOITEWA

2306; [Blank]; m; 79 (1853); F; m; Head; yes; yes; E
2307; Sonwyeh; f; 68 (1864); F; m; wife; yes; yes; E

TEEMU

2308; Myra; f; 47 (1905); F; w; Head; yes; yes; F
2309; Bruce; m; 9 (1923); F; s; son; yes; yes; F
2310; Harold; m; 7 (1925); F; s; son; yes; yes; F
2311; Gilbert; m; 5 (10-25-26); F; s; son; yes; yes; F

2312; Porter; m; 29 (1903); F; m; Head; yes; yes; F

TEHLAKHONGEVA

2313; Lloyd; m; 30 (1902); F; m; Head; yes; yes; I
2314; Selma; f; 30 (1902); F; m; wife; yes; yes; I
2315; Uberta; f; ?; f; s; dau; yes; yes; I
2316; Bert; m; 3 (1929); F; s; son; yes; yes; I
2317; Virginia; f; 3/12 (12-28-31); F; s; dau; yes; yes; I

TEVANUKEOMA

2318; [Blank]; m; 63 (1869); F; m; Head; yes; yes; D
2319; Nuvawensie; f; 60 (1872); F; m; wife; yes; yes; D
2320; **Eptavi**, Isaac; m; 38 (1894); F; s; son; yes; yes; D
2321; **Opoh**, Arthur; m; 27 (1905); F; s; grnd-son; yes; yes; D
2322; **Honwynema**, Maybelle; f; 20 (1912); F; s; grnd-dau; yes; yes; D
2323; **Honwynema**, Emerson; m; 1 (1930); F; s; g-g-son; yes; yes; D
2324; **Honamanema**, Angeline; f; 19 (1913); F; s; grnd-dau; yes; yes; D
2325; **Jawanheftewa**, Tom; m; 13 (1919); F; s; grnd-son; yes; yes; D
2326; **Jawanheftewa**, Eunice; f; 11 (1921); F; s; grnd-dau; yes; yes; D

TEWAHEFTEWA

2327; [Blank]; m; 71 (1861); F; m; Head; yes; yes; F
2328; [Blank]; f; 72 (1860); F; m; wife; yes; yes; F
2329; **Lomaltestewa**, [Blank]; m; 91 (1841); F; w; uncle; yes; yes; F

HOPI INDIAN CENSUS, (As of April 1, 1932)

KEY: Census Number; Name; Sex; Age at Last Birthday; Tribe (Hopi, unless otherwise stated); Degree of Blood; Marital Status; Relationship to Head of Family; At Jurisdiction where enrolled [Yes or No] (If no, Where); Ward [Yes or No]; Hopi Village [according to key].

TEWANMANEWA

2330; Doc; m; 53 (1879); F; m; Head; yes; yes; F
2331; Maude; f; 41 (1891); F; m; wife; yes; yes; F
2332; Esther; f; 23 (1909); F; s; dau; yes; yes; F
2333; Ross; m; 20 (1920); F; s; son; yes; yes; F
2334; Elizabeth; f; 16 (1916); F; s; dau; yes; yes; F
2335; Tessie; f; 6 (1926); F; s; dau; yes; yes; F

TEWANAYUMPTEWA

2336; [Blank]; m; 59 (1873); F; m; Head; yes; yes; I
2337; Sehongumum; f; 57 (1875); F; m; wife; yes; yes; I
2338; Joel; m; 21 (1911); F; s; son; yes; yes; I
2339; Marie; f; 16 (1916); F; s; dau; yes; yes; I
2340; Eleanor; f; 14 (1918); F; s; dau; yes; yes; I

TEWANEMA

2341; Louis; m; 50 (1882); F; m; Head; yes; yes; F
2342; Blanche; m; 47 (1885); F; m; wife; yes; yes; F

TEWANIMPTEWA

2343; Dennis; m; 50 (1882); F; m; Head; yes; yes; D
2344; Uvenaka; f; 50 (1882); F; m; wife; yes; yes; D
2345; **Sohuh**, Alec; m; 27 (1905); F; m; son; yes; yes; D
2346; **Koyanifikeoma**, Chester; m; 23 (1909); F; s; son; yes; yes; D
2347; **Puhyowma**, Emory; m; 19 (1913); F; s; son; yes; yes; D
2348; **Secaventewa**, Leland; m; 18 (1914); F; s; son; yes; yes; D
2349; **Queveletstewa**, Elwood; m; 15 (1917); F; s; son; yes; yes; yes; D
2350; Edith; f; 12 (1920); F; s; dau; yes; yes; D
2351; **Kawyyo**, Norbert; m; 6 (1926); F; s; son; yes; yes; D

TEWANIMPTEWA

2352; [Blank]; m; 68 (1864); F; w; Head; yes; yes; F
2353; Seymour; m; 35 (1897); F; s; nephew; yes; yes; F

TEWAWINO

2354; Pat; m; 52 (1880); F; m; Head; yes; yes; F
2355; Effie; f; 38 (1894); F; m; wife; yes; yes; F
2356; Marcia; f; 19 (1913); F; s; dau; yes; yes; F

KEY: Census Number; Name; Sex; Age at Last Birthday; Tribe (Hopi, unless otherwise stated); Degree of Blood; Marital Status; Relationship to Head of Family; At Jurisdiction where enrolled [Yes or No] (If no, Where); Ward [Yes or No]; Hopi Village [according to key].

2357; Pershing; m; 10 (1922); F; s; son; yes; yes; F
2358; Waldine; f; 8 (1924); F; s; dau; yes; yes; F
2359; Elfrieda; f; 6 (3-29-26); F; s; dau; yes; yes; F
2360; Wilford; m; 3 (1-20-29); F; s; son; yes; yes; F

THOMPSON

2361; Vina; f; 43 (1889); F; w; Head; yes; yes; G

TOGIE

2362; [Blank]; m; 62 (1870); F; w; Head; yes; yes; B

TOMASSO

2363; Timothy; m; 27 (1905); F; m; Head; yes; yes; A
2364; Laura; f; 25 (1907); F; m; wife; yes; yes; A

TONGEVIS

2365; Ritherford; m; 43 (1889); F; w; Head; yes; yes; F
2366; Alexander; m; 22 (1910); F; s; son; yes; yes; F
2367; Hazel; f; 19 (1913); F; s; dau; yes; yes; F

TONGOCKWISNOMA

2368; [Blank]; m; 51 (1881); F; m; Head; yes; yes; A
2369; Pahlah; f; 45 (1887); F; m; wife; yes; yes; A
2370; **Palaquota**, Lidge; m; 29 (1903); F; s; son; yes; yes; A
2371; Luke; m; 27 (1905); F; s; son; yes; yes; A

TONOCKHONGOVA

2372; [Blank]; m; 57 (1875); F; m; Head; yes; yes; I
2373; Sinimka; f; 55 (1877); F; m; wife; yes; yes; I
2374; Samuel; m; 23 (1909); F; s; son; yes; yes; I

TOONEWAH

2375; [Blank]; m; 57 (1875); F; m; Head; yes; yes; C
2376; Sally; f; 53 (1879); F; m; wife; yes; yes; C
2377; Pat; m; 28 (1904); F; s; son; yes; yes; C
2378; Marcia; f; 16 (1916); F; s; dau; yes; yes; C
2379; Guy Miller; m; 10 (1922); F; s; son; yes; yes; C

HOPI INDIAN CENSUS, (As of April 1, 1932)

KEY: Census Number; Name; Sex; Age at Last Birthday; Tribe (Hopi, unless otherwise stated); Degree of Blood; Marital Status; Relationship to Head of Family; At Jurisdiction where enrolled [Yes or No] (If no, Where); Ward [Yes or No]; Hopi Village [according to key].

TOUHMA

2380; Jacob; m; 42 (1890); F; m; Head; yes; yes; D
2381; (Seyownema), Jean; f; 33 (1899); F; m; wife; yes; yes; D
2382; Daniel; m; 14 (1918); F; s; son; yes; yes; D
2383; Marie; f; 12 (1920:; F; s; dau; yes; yes; D
2384; Pereival; m; 11 (1921); F; s; son; yes; yes; D
2385; Rosemary; f; 8 (1924); F; s; dau; yes; yes; D
2386; Jenness; f; 5 (4-25-26); F; s; dau; yes; yes; D
2387; Mary Elizabeth; f; 3 (2-27-29); F; s; dau; yes; yes; D
2388; Richard; m; 1 (3-29-31); F; s; son; yes; yes; D
2389; **Nahutewa**, [Blank]; m; 81 (1851); F; w; father-in-law; yes; yes; D

TOWONGNINEMA

2390; [Blank]; f; 57 (1875); F; w; Head; yes; yes; B
2391; Marian; f; 20 (1912); F; s; dau; yes; yes; B
2392; Sunbeam; f; 17 (1915); F; s; dau; yes; yes; B

TSORSHOIMOMA

2393; [Blank]; f; 71 (1861); F; w; Head; yes; yes; G

TUBAKINA

2394; Smiley; m; 32 (1900); F; m; Head; yes; yes; C
2395; Marjorie; f; 26 (1906); F; m; wife; yes; yes; C
2396; Richard; m; 3 (5-4-28); F; s; son; yes; yes; C
2397; Rosalie; f; 2 (1-10-30); F; s; dau; yes; yes; C
2398; Bennett; m; 5/12 (10-16-31); F; s; son; yes; yes; C

TUOAPA

2399; [Blank]; m; 38 (1894); F; s; Head; yes; yes; G

TUVAHAPNOM

2400; Mary; f; 65 (1867); F; w; Head; yes; yes; G
2401; Ross; m; 34 (1898); F; s; son; yes; yes; G
2402; Clay; m; 31 (1901); F; s; son; yes; yes; G

TUVAQUAPTEWA

2403; Gilbert; m; 52 (1880); F; m; Head; yes; yes; I

KEY: Census Number; Name; Sex; Age at Last Birthday; Tribe (Hopi, unless otherwise stated); Degree of Blood; Marital Status; Relationship to Head of Family; At Jurisdiction where enrolled [Yes or No] (If no, Where); Ward [Yes or No]; Hopi Village [according to key].

2404; (Tuvunimka), [Blank]; f; 49 (1883); F; m; wife; yes; yes; I
2405; **Masahewnim**, Myrtle; f; 17 (1915); F; s; stp-dau; yes; yes; I

TUVEHOYIWMA

2406; [Blank]; m; 65 (1867); F; m; Head; yes; yes; G
2407; Susie; f; 57 (1875); F; m; wife; yes; yes; G
2408; Kyrat; m; 19 (1913); F; s; son; yes; yes; G
2409; Ilene; f; 11 (1921); F; s; dau; yes; yes; G
2410; Ray; m; 34 (1898); F; s; stp-son; yes; yes; G
2411; Jean; m; 21 (1911); F; s; stp-son; yes; yes; G

TUVENOMTIWA

2412; [Blank]; m; 70 (1862); F; m; Head; yes; yes; G
2413; Fannie; f; 68 (1864); F; m; wife; yes; yes; G
2414; Inez; f; 23 (1909); F; s; dau; yes; yes; G

TUVEYAMTIWA

2415; [Blank]; m; 81 (1851); F; w; Head; yes; yes; G
2416; Dorothy; f; 23 (1909); F; s; grnd-dau; yes; yes; G

TUWAHNEWA

2417; Henry; m; 27 (1905); F; m; Head; yes; yes; I
2418; (Tanakeyowma), Alma; f; 24 (1908); F; m; wife; yes; yes; I
2419; [Blank]; (?); 4/12 (11-14-31); F; s; (?); yes; yes; I

TYMA

2420; Lewis; m; 30 (1902); F; m; Head; yes; yes; F
2421; Josie; f; 27 (1905); F; m; wife; yes; yes; F
2422; Gladys; f; 8 (1924); F; s; dau; yes; yes; F
2423; Byron; m; 8/12 (7-27-31); F; s; son; yes; yes; F

UYOUNGEVA

2424; Henry; m; 28 (1894); F; m; Head; yes; yes; D
2425; (Sewingonisie), Carrie; f; 29 (1903); F; m; wife; yes; yes; D
2426; [Unnamed]; m; (?); F; s; son; yes; yes; D

KEY: Census Number; Name; Sex; Age at Last Birthday; Tribe (Hopi, unless otherwise stated); Degree of Blood; Marital Status; Relationship to Head of Family; At Jurisdiction where enrolled [Yes or No] (If no, Where); Ward [Yes or No]; Hopi Village [according to key].

VENICE

2427; [Blank]; m; 83 (1849); F; w; Head; yes; yes; C

VENTEWA

2428; Albert; m; 49 (1883); F; m; Head; yes; yes; I
2429; Gashwynim; f; ?; F; m; wife; yes; yes; I
2430; Vaughan; m; 3 (8-12-29); F; s; son; yes; yes; I
2431; Alanson; m; 3/12 (1-1-32); F; s; son; yes; yes; I
2432; Bert; m; ?; F; s; stp-son; yes; yes; I
2433; Gordon; m; 12 (1920); F; s; stp-son; yes; yes; I
2434; Corrina; f; ?; F; s; stp-dau; yes; yes; I

WAZRA

2435; Taylor; m; 38 (1894); F; m; Head; yes; yes; F
2436; Lily; f; 42 (1890); F; m; wife; yes; yes; F
2437; Lillian; f; 21 (1911); F; s; dau; yes; yes; F
2438; Rosilind; f; 14 (1918); F; s; dau; yes; yes; F
2439; Viola; f; 12 (1920); F; s; dau; yes; yes; F
2440; Louise; f; 9 (1923); F; s; dau; yes; yes; F
2441; Dalton; m; 5 (9-19-26); F; s; son; yes; yes; F

2442; [Blank]; m; 56 (1976); F; m; Head; yes; yes; B
2443; Longley; f; 54 (1878); F; m; wife; yes; yes; B
2444; Freida; f; 14 (1918); F; s; dau; yes; yes; B

WEAKEMA

2445; Teddy; m; 33 (1899); F; m; Head; yes; yes; A
2446; Patty; f; 31 (1901); F; m; wife; yes; yes; A

WELLINGTON

2447; Laura; f; 49 (1883); F; w; Head; yes; yes; G
2448; Lloyd; m; 22 (1910); F; s; son; yes; yes; G
2449; Dorothy; f; 20 (1912); F; s; dau; yes; yes; G
2450; Joshua; m; 10 (1922); F; s; son; yes; yes; G

WIKI

2451; Paul; m; 47 (1885); F; w; Head; yes; yes; C
2452; Mary; f; 20 (1912); F; s; dau; yes; yes; C

KEY: Census Number; Name; Sex; Age at Last Birthday; Tribe (Hopi, unless otherwise stated); Degree of Blood; Marital Status; Relationship to Head of Family; At Jurisdiction where enrolled [Yes or No] (If no, Where); Ward [Yes or No]; Hopi Village [according to key].

2453; Josiah; m; 18 (1914); F; s; son; yes; yes; C
2454; Ethel; f; 5 (1927); F; s; dau; yes; yes; C

WINNUTAH

2455; [Blank]; f; 67 (1865); F; w; Head; yes; yes; C

WOPTAWA

2456; Perry; m; 29 (1903); F; m; Head; yes; yes; E
2457; (Sekanguimpka), Elsie; f; 27 (1905); F; m; wife; yes; yes; E
2458; Perry Joseph; m; 3 (1929); F; s; son; yes; yes; E

WUNGNEWA

459; Ernest; m; 34 (1898); F; m; Head; yes; yes; I
2460; Vera; f; 30 (1902); F; m; wife; yes; yes; I
2461; Bernice; f; 6 (1926); F; s; dau; yes; yes; I
2462; Burton; m; 3 (5-5-28); F; s; son; yes; yes; I
2463; Randall; m; 2 (1930); F; s; son; yes; yes; I

WYTEWA

2464; Benjamin; m; 39 (1893); F; w; Head; yes; yes; I

YAIVA

2465; Seth; m; 40 (1892); F; m; Head; no; Insane Asylum, P.O. Phoenix, Pinal Co, AZ; yes; H
2466; Elsie; f; 39 (1893); F; m; wife; yes; yes; H
2467 Joel; m; 17 (1915); F; s; son; yes; yes; H
2468; Leonard; m; 12 (1920); F; s; son; yes; yes; H
2469; Travis; m; 10 (1922); F; s; son; yes; yes; H
2470; Lydia; f; 8 (1924); F; s; dau; yes; yes; H
2471; Hurst; m; 6 (1926); F; s; son; yes; yes; H
2472; Byron; m; 1 (1930); F; s; son; yes; yes; H

YAVA

2473; Albert; m; 42 (1890); F; m; Head; yes; yes; A
2474; Tayomana; f; 44 (1888); F; m; wife; yes; yes; A
2475; Juanita; f; 16 (1916); F; s; dau; yes; yes; A
2476; Patricia; f; 13 (1919) F; s; dau; yes; yes; A
2477; Sarah; f; 13 (1920); F; s; dau; yes; yes; A

KEY: Census Number; Name; Sex; Age at Last Birthday; Tribe (Hopi, unless otherwise stated); Degree of Blood; Marital Status; Relationship to Head of Family; At Jurisdiction where enrolled [Yes or No] (If no, Where); Ward [Yes or No]; Hopi Village [according to key].

2478; **Massah**, Tom; m; 25 (1907); F; s; son; yes; yes; A
2479; **Massah**, Woodrow; m; 19 (1913); f; s; son; yes; yes; A
2480; **Massah**, Ethel; f; 16 (1916); F; s; dau; yes; yes; A

YESTEWA

2481; Herbert; m; 45 (1889); F m; Head; yes; yes; G
2482; Dell; f; 43 (1889); F; m; wife; yes; yes; G
2483; Paul; m; 20 (1912); F; s; son; yes; yes; G

YOUKTI

2484; Frances; f; 39 (1893); F; w; Head; yes; yes; C
2485; Norma Frances; f; 8 (1924); F; s; dau; yes; yes; C

YOUNGNOIUMA

2486; Luke; m; 31 (1901); F; m; Head; yes; yes; A
2487; Myrtle; f; 29 (1903); F; m; wife; yes; yes; A
2488; Iver; m; 9 (1923); F; s; son; yes; yes; A
2489; Enid; f; 8 (1924); F; s; dau; yes; yes; A
2490; Harriet; f; 4 (11-10-27); F; s; dau; yes; yes; A

YOUVELLA

2491; Bert; m; 42 (1890); F; m; Head; yes; yes; A
2492; Belle; f; 42 (1890); F; m; wife; yes; yes; A
2493; Roy; m; 19 (1913); F; s; son; yes; yes; A
2494; Charley; m; 16 (1916); F; s; dau; yes; yes; A
2495; Harry; m; 15 (1917); F; s; son; yes; yes; A
2496; Ethel; f; 13 (1919); F; s; dau; yes; yes; A
2497; Mildred; f; 10 (1922); F; s; dau; yes; yes; A

YOUWITCHQUAMA

2498; Bishop; m; 37 (1895); F; w; Head; yes; yes; F
2499; Zelma; f; 15 (1917); F; s; dau; yes; yes; F

YOUYUWYYA

2500; Dennis N; m; 29 (1903); F; m; Head; yes; yes; A
2501; Mamie; f; 26 (1906); F; m; wife; yes; yes; A
2502; Gazelle; f; 1 (11-19-30); F; s; dau; yes; yes; A

KEY: Census Number; Name; Sex; Age at Last Birthday; Tribe (Hopi, unless otherwise stated); Degree of Blood; Marital Status; Relationship to Head of Family; At Jurisdiction where enrolled [Yes or No] (If no, Where); Ward [Yes or No]; Hopi Village [according to key].

YOYOWTEWA

2503; Mack; m; 58 (1874); F; m; Head; yes; yes; F
2504; Alice; f; 61 (1871); F; m; wife; yes; yes; F
2505; Lily; f; 17 (1915); F; s; dau; yes; yes; F
2506; Raymond; m; 16 (1916); F; s; son; yes; yes; F
2507; Russel; m; 15 (1917); F; s; son; yes; yes; F

2508; (Mootaka), Daisy; f; ?; F; w; Head; yes; yes; F
2509; Winifred; f; 9/12 (6-19-31); F; s; dau; yes; yes; F

YOYOHONGAVA

2510; Barney; m; 57 (1875); F; m; Head; yes; yes; F
2511; Ethel; f; 58 (1874); F; m; wife; yes; yes; F
2512; Molly; f; 19 (1913); F; s; dau; yes; yes; F

YOYOWAYTIWA

2513; Richard; m; 40 (1892); F; m; Head; yes; yes; G
2514; Mabel; f; 29 (1903); F; m; wife; yes; yes; G
2515; Arthur; m; 11 (1921); F; s; son; yes; yes; G
2516; Earl; m; 9 (1923); F; s; son; yes; yes; G
2517; **Mazie**, Lillian; f; 4 (5-10-27); F; s; dau; yes; yes; G

ZEENA

2518; Richard; m; 37 (1895); F; m; Head; yes; yes; B
2519; Esther; f; 30 (1902); F; m; wife; yes; yes; B
2520; Ned; m; 12 (1920); F; s; son; yes; yes; B
2521; Marylin; f; 3 (5-19-28); F; s; dau; yes; yes; B
2522; Martha; f; 1 (1-17-31); F; s; dau; yes; yes; B

ZEYOUMA

2523; Philip; m; 39 (1893); F; m; Head; yes; yes; D
2524; Philip, Jr; m; 18 (1914); F; s; son; yes; yes; D
2525; Gladys; f; 13 (1919); F; s; dau; yes; yes; D
2526; Charlotte; f; 12 (1920); F; s; dau; yes; yes; D
2527; Thelma; f; 10 (1922); F; s; dau; yes; yes; D
2528; Alfonso; m; 7 (1925); F; s; son; yes; yes; D
2529; Faye; f; 1 (1930); F; s; dau; yes; yes; D

KEY: Census Number; Name; Sex; Age at Last Birthday; Tribe (Hopi, unless otherwise stated); Degree of Blood; Marital Status; Relationship to Head of Family; At Jurisdiction where enrolled [Yes or No] (If no, Where); Ward [Yes or No]; Hopi Village [according to key].

ZOSHROKTEIOMA

2530; Hurst; m; 35 (1897); F; m; Head; yes; yes; D

2531; (Quahonema), Eva; f; 29 (1903); F; m; wife; yes; yes; D

2532; Harvey; m; 9 (1923); F; s; son; yes; yes; D

2533; Kirkland; m; 7 (1925); F; s; son; yes; yes; D

2534; Vera; f; 3 (1929); F; s; dau; yes; yes; D

2535; Lolita; f; 1 (10-25-30); F; s; dau; yes; yes; D

2536; **Tahlumpa**, Martin; m; 15 (1917); F; s; bro-in-law; yes; yes; D

2537; **Kewanwynema**, Grace; f; 12 (1920); F; s; sis-in-law; yes; yes; D

2538; **Kewanwynema**, Warren; m; 10 (1922); F; s; bro-in-law; yes; yes; D

LIVE BIRTHS

of the

HOPI TRIBE

Hopi Indian Agency

Keams Canon,

Arizona 1925 - 1931

KEY: 1931 Census Roll Number ("----" indicates no number given); Name; Date of Birth; Sex; Tribe (Hopi, unless otherwise indicated); Ward [yes or no]; Degree of Father's blood; Degree of Mother's blood; Degree of Child's blood; At jurisdiction where enrolled [yes or no]; (If "no", where?).

----;   ADAMS, Laura; 8-16-1930; f; yes; F; F; F; yes

  14;   ADAMS, Roberta; 9-10-1930; f; yes; F; F; F yes

  42;   AHMI, Bettie; 10-13-1930; f; yes; F; F; F; yes

----;   AHOWONA, Thomas; 2-3-1931; m; yes; F; F; F; yes

----;   BAKURZA, Zella; 7-15-1930; f; yes; F; F; F; yes

----;   CALEMYTEWA, David; 11-9-1930; m; yes; F; F; F; yes

 166;   CHUAHYOWMA, Lois Evalyn; 8-20-1930; f; yes; F; F; F; yes

 258;   DEWITT, Frances; 12-11-1930; f; yes; F; F; F; yes

 271;   DOUMA, Zella; 10-1-1930; f; yes; F; F; F; yes

 301;   DUWAHONGVA, Edith; 7-5-1930; f; yes; F; F; F; yes

 305;   DUWAKUKU, Myrtle; 9-15-1930; f; yes; F; F; F; yes

 422;   HARRIS, Eric; 9-10-1030; m; yes; F; F; F; yes

 428;   HARVEY, Milton; 3-21-1931; m; yes; F; F; F; yes

 475;   HOMANA, Walter; 10-23-1930; m; yes; F; F; F; yes

 484;   HOMEWYTEWA, Adeline; 2-15-1931; f; yes; F; F; F; yes

----;   HONANIA. Harriett Alice; 1-6-1931; f; yes; F; F; F; yes

 531;   HONUMPTIE, Elvira; 7-11-1930; f; yes; F; F; F; yes

----;   HOWATO, Raymond Charles; 1-22-1931; m; yes; F; F; F; yes

 601;   JAMES, Caroline; 7-7-1930; f; yes; F; F; F; yes

 660;   KARZOH, Laila Lee; 12-14-1930; f; yes; F; F; F; yes

----;   KOINVE, Samuel; 8-15-1930; m; yes; F; F; F; yes

 881;   LACAPA, Bennett; 2-6-1931; m; yes; F; F; F; yes

LIVE BIRTHS, (Occurring between April 1, 1930, and March 31, 1931)
KEY: 1931 Census Roll Number ("----" indicates no number given); Name; Date of Birth; Sex; Tribe (Hopi, unless otherwise indicated); Ward [yes or no]; Degree of Father's blood; Degree of Mother's blood; Degree of Child's blood; At jurisdiction where enrolled [yes or no]; (If "no", where?).

908; LANSA, Edward; 2-12-1931; m; yes; F; F; F; yes

973; LOMAKEMA, Luther; 11-11-1930; m; yes; F; F; F; yes

----; LOMASNEWA, Leroy; 8-27-1930; m; yes; F; F; F; yes

1161; MASANIMPTEWA, Mollie; 10-1-1930; f; yes; F; F; F; yes

1154; MASKEEF, Emma; 2-25-1931; f; yes; F; F; F; yes

1245; NAHSONHOYO, Neal; 10-27-1930; m; yes; F; F; F; yes

1253; NAMINGHA, Elinor; 10-12-1930; f; yes; F; F; F; yes

1308; NAVAMSA, Pelavera; 11-13-1930; f; yes; F; F; F; yes

----; [No Name]; 11-16-1930; m; yes; F; F; F; yes   Child of Roland Nehoitewa

1348; NEVAYKTEWA, Vina; 1-29-1931; f; yes; F; F; F; yes

----; NICHOLAS, Mary S; 8-18-1930; f; yes; F; F; F; yes

1407; ONSAY, Roland; 3-31-1931; m; yes; F; F; F; yes

1521; POHONA, Lulu; 3-26-1931; f; yes; F; F; F; yes

1584; POLILANEMA, Webster; 9-12-1930; m; yes; F; F; F; yes

1649; POOLA, Mitchell; 3-7-1931; m; yes; F; F; F; yes

1459; POVATEA, Dick; 9-26-1930; m; yes; F; F; F; yes

1696; QAKWANWA, Roderick; 3-18-1931; m; yes; F; F; F; yes

1742; QUAVEHEMA, Iola; 8-5-1930; f; yes; F; F; F; yes

----; SAYAHMA, Gerald Moyer; 1-10-1931; m; yes; F; F; F; yes

1935; SEEZRO, Eldon; 10-6-1930; m; yes; F; F; F; yes

----; SEKATAYOU, Dora; 9-13-1930; f; yes; F; F; F; yes

2007; SEQUI, Everett; 11-18-1930; m; yes; F; F; F; yes

100

LIVE BIRTHS, (Occurring between April 1, 1930, and March 31, 1931)
KEY: 1931 Census Roll Number ("----" indicates no number given); Name; Date of Birth; Sex; Tribe (Hopi, unless otherwise indicated); Ward [yes or no]; Degree of Father's blood; Degree of Mother's blood; Degree of Child's blood; At jurisdiction where enrolled [yes or no]; (If "no", where?).

2037;   SHELTON, Betsy; 3-20-1931; f; yes; F; F; F; yes

----;   SHULACHIVIE, Vann; 12-20-1930; m; yes; F; F; F; yes

2060;   SIHEIMA, Frank; 12-16-1930; m; yes; F; F; F; yes

----;   SINGYOWMA, Mary Louise; 10-19-1930; yes; F; F; F; yes

----;   SMITH, Elsie; 6-11-1931; f; yes; F; F; F; yes

2214;   TALAWISUMA, Annabel; 3-10-1931; f; yes; F; F; F; yes

2154;   TALOS, Margaret; 9-24-1930; f; yes; F; F; F; yes

----;   TEEMU, Tilman; 12-2-1930; m; yes; ?; F; ½; yes

----;   TEEMU, Travis; 12-2-1930; m; yes; ?; F; ½; yes

2321;   TEWAWINO, Mahoney; 12-2-1930; m; yes; F; F; F; yes

2349;   TOUHMA, Richard; 3-29-1931; m; yes; F; F; F; yes

2457;   YOUYUWYYA, Gazella; 11-19-1930; ?; yes; F; F; F; yes

2376;   ZEENA, Martha; 1-17-1931; f; yes; F; F; F; yes

2489;   ZOSHROKTEIOMA, Lolita; 10-25-1930; f; yes; F; F; F; yes

LIVE BIRTHS, (Occurring between July 1, 1929, and June 30, 1930)

KEY: 1930 Census Roll Number ("----" indicates no number given); Name; Date of Birth; Sex; Tribe (Hopi, unless otherwise indicated); Ward [yes or no]; Degree of Father's blood; Degree of Mother's blood; Degree of Child's blood; At jurisdiction where enrolled [yes or no]; (If "no", where?).

4;   ADAMS, Lorna; 9-21-1929; f; yes; F; F; F; yes

5;   ALBERT, Lynn; 8-1-1929; f; yes; F; F; F; yes

15;   BATALA, Percy; 8-13-1929; m; yes; F; F; F; yes

93;   BATANHOYA, Lanora Martha; 6-26-1930; f; yes; F; F; F; yes
(Number is 1931 Roll #)

----;   CHACA, Joseph; 4-3-1930; m; yes; F; F; F; yes

127;   CHEKUMIE, Nona; 2-15-1930; f; yes; F; F; F; yes
(Number is 1931 Roll #)

----;   CHEWATEWA, Suzanne Rink; 6-13-1930; f; yes; F; F; F; yes

----;   CHEYKOYOHI, Lloyd; 2-28-1930; m; yes; ?; F; ½; yes

12;   CHICUEOMA, Donald; 11-5-1929; m; yes; F; F; F; yes

----;   COOKA, Tom Cruse; 6-28-1930; m; yes; F; F; F; yes

47;   DASHEE, Loraine; 4-20-1930; f; yes; F; F; F; yes

* 15;   DAVID, Ethel Ryan; 7-7-1929; f; yes; F; F; F; yes *(*NOTE: # given twice)*

----;   DOWAHOYA, Reuben; 5-27-1930; m; yes; F; F; F; yes

----;   DUERCHE, Magdalena Rose; 8-16-1929; f; yes; F; F; F; yes

81;   GAHLAH, (Blank); 7-27-1929; f; yes; F; F; F; no; Santa Anita, CA.

----;   GASHQUAPNIM, Monroe; 10-31-1929; m; yes; ?; F; ½; yes

27;   HONANI, Dora; 4-9-1930; f; yes; F; F; F; yes

----;   HONHONGAVA, Stephen; 12-10-1929; m; yes; F; F; F; yes

522;   HONWATEWA, Louis Calvin; 6-30-1930; m; yes; F; F; F; yes
(Number is 1931 Roll #)

----;   HOWOTO, Bennett; 11-7-1929; m; yes; F; F; F; yes

102

LIVE BIRTHS, (Occurring between July 1, 1929, and June 30, 1930)

KEY: 1930 Census Roll Number ("----" indicates no number given); Name; Date of Birth; Sex; Tribe (Hopi, unless otherwise indicated); Ward [yes or no]; Degree of Father's blood; Degree of Mother's blood; Degree of Child's blood; At jurisdiction where enrolled [yes or no]; (If "no", where?).

----;   HOWOTO, Russell; 11-7-1929; m; yes; F; F; F; yes

546;   HOYUNGWA, Robert; 4-19-1930; m; yes; F; F; F; yes
(Number is 1931 Roll #)

----;   HUMATEWA, Leland; 7-29-1929; m; yes; F; F; F; yes

 28;   HYEOMA, Lydia; 11-23-1929; f; yes; F; F; F; yes

125;   JENKINS, Peter; 2-2-1930; m; yes; F; F; F; yes

136;   JOHNSON, Viena; 11-1-1929; f; yes; F; F; F; yes

----;   KAEHMANNA, Cleo; 11-1-1929; f; yes; ?; F; ½; yes

----;   KEWANEMA, Hazel; 8-28-1929; f; yes; F; F; F; yes

----;   KOOYAQUAPTEWA, Edgar; 3-18-1930; m; yes; F; F; F; yes

----;   KORUH, Amy; 4-25-1930; f; yes; F; F; F; yes

888;   LAHPOO, Mavis; 6-15-1930; f; yes; F; F; F; yes
(Number is 1931 Roll #)

----;   LANSA, Anna May; 9-1-1929; f; yes; F; F; F; yes

916;   LESLIE, Cynthia; 6-1-1930; f; yes; F; F; F; yes
(Number is 1931 Roll #)

163;   LOMAHEPTEWA, Mark; 4-1-1930; m; yes; F; F; F; yes

----;   LOMAYESTEWA, Martin; 4-1-1930; m; yes; F; F; F; yes

201;   LOMAYASVA, Ruth Talas; 10-5-1929; f; yes; F; F; F; yes

----;   MABLE, Verla; 5-16-1930; f; yes; F; F; F; yes

132;   MAHTSWONGNE, Thana; 11-5-1929; f; yes; F; F; F; yes

228;   MASAYANTIWA, Lois; 4-24-1930; f; yes; F; F; F; yes

213;   MONNONGE, Dollie; 3-1-1930; f; yes; F; F; F; yes

103

LIVE BIRTHS, (Occurring between July 1, 1929, and June 30, 1930)
KEY: 1930 Census Roll Number ("----" indicates no number given); Name; Date of Birth; Sex; Tribe (Hopi, unless otherwise indicated); Ward [yes or no]; Degree of Father's blood; Degree of Mother's blood; Degree of Child's blood; At jurisdiction where enrolled [yes or no]; (If "no", where?).

138; MOOETWA, Bernard; 3-31-1930; m; yes; F; F; F; yes

1203; NAHA, Albert; 9-1-1929; m; yes; F; F; F; yes
(Number is 1931 Roll #)

156; NAHA, Ray; 12-5-1929; m; yes; F; F; F; yes

1218; NAHE, Naomi; 6-24-1930; f; yes; F; F; F; yes
(Number is 1931 Roll #)

169; NAVAKUKU, Mary Anna; 5-19-1930; f; yes; F; F; F; yes

200; NAYATEWA, Sara Lorena; 7-31-1929; f; yes; F; F; F; yes

----; NEVOUNGIATEWA, Hilda; 9-22-1929; f; yes; F; F; F; yes

118; NUMKEMA, Rena; 10-3-1929; f; yes; F; F; F; yes

1398; NUTUMYA, Eloise; 4-19-1930; f; yes; F; F; F; yes
(Number is 1931 Roll #)

124; OHKOWYA, Delphine; 5-24-1930; f; yes; F; F; F; yes

----; OUTAH, Elson; 6-7-1930; m; yes; F; F; F; yes

----; OYAPING, Judith Anna; 4-1-1930; f; yes; F; F; F; yes

----; PENTEWA, Annie; 1-3-1930; f; yes; F; F; F; yes

81; PESHOKTEOMA, Lawrence; 1-13-1930; m; yes; F; F; F; yes

208; POLACCA, Harold; 10-18-1929; m; yes; F; F; F; yes

202; POLACCA, Miriam; 11-7-1929; f; yes; F; F; F; yes

----; POLACCA, Thelma; 11-15-1929; f; yes; F; F; F; yes

206; POLINGYOWMA, Glenna; 3-4-1930; f; yes; F; F; F; yes

236; POOCHA, Margie Inez; 3-26-1930; f; yes; F; F; F; yes

304; POOYOUMA, Fletcher; 8-27-1929; m; yes; F; F; F; yes

KEY: 1930 Census Roll Number ("----" indicates no number given); Name; Date of Birth; Sex; Tribe (Hopi, unless otherwise indicated); Ward [yes or no]; Degree of Father's blood; Degree of Mother's blood; Degree of Child's blood; At jurisdiction where enrolled [yes or no]; (If "no", where?).

----; POSEYESVA, Charles Raymond; 12-23-1929; m; yes; F; F; F; yes

212; POVATAH, Calvin; 1-26-1930; m; yes; F; F; F; yes

242; QUIQUA, Margaret; 1-23-1930; f; yes; F; F; F; yes

240; SEECHONE, Robert Edward; 11-15-1929; m; yes; F; F; F; yes

177; SECLETSTEWA, Frances; 3-9-1930; f; yes; F; F; F; yes

1951; SEKAQUAPTEWA, Abbott; 12-4-1929; m; yes; F; F; F; yes
(Number is 1931 Roll #)

358; SEKIUOUMA, Ethel; 11-11-1929; f; yes; F; F; F; yes

----; SEMEHONA, Erma; 5-3-1930; f; yes; F; F; F; yes

----; SEKATAYOU, Leon; 6-4-1930; m; yes; F; F; F; yes

269; SHUPULA, Leonard; 11-17-1929; m; yes; F; F; F; yes

2087; SILAS, Judith; 6-26-1930; f; yes; F; F; F; yes
(Number is 1931 Roll #)

92; SOCQUESVIA, Evert; 12-5-1929; m; yes; F; F; F; yes

2114; SUETOPKA, Esther; 11-14-1929; f; yes; F; F; F; yes
(Number is 1931 Roll #)

2142; TAHO, Elbert; 6-26-1930; m; yes; F; F; F; yes
(Number is 1931 Roll #)

----; TAKALA, Owen; 8-2-1929; m; yes; F; F; F; yes

----; TALAUMOTEWA, Stella; 9-23-1929; f; yes; F; F; F; yes

246; TALAWISUMA, Vincent; 9-1-1929; m; yes; F; F; F; yes

255; TALAYUMPTEWA, Sadie; 4-22-1930; f; yes; F; F; F; yes

----; TENEKHONGVA, Bert; 12-6-1929; m; yes; F; F; F; yes

----; THOMAS, Eloise; 1-7-1930; f; yes; F; F; F; yes

LIVE BIRTHS, (Occurring between July 1, 1929, and June 30, 1930)
KEY: 1930 Census Roll Number ("----" indicates no number given); Name; Date of Birth; Sex; Tribe (Hopi, unless otherwise indicated); Ward [yes or no]; Degree of Father's blood; Degree of Mother's blood; Degree of Child's blood; At jurisdiction where enrolled [yes or no]; (If "no", where?).

----;   TOPHONGNIM, Vera; 3-31-1930; f; yes; ?; F; ½; yes

154;   TUBIKEMA, Rosalie; 1-10-1930; f; yes; F; F; F; yes

408;   VENTEWA, Vaughn; 8-12-1929; m; yes; F; F; F; yes

----;   YOUNGNOIUMA, Lolita; 9-17-1929; f; yes; F; F; F; yes

----;   YOUYUWYYA, Laura; 11-1-1929; f; yes; F; F; F; yes

----;   YOVWETEWA, Edward; 2-21-1930; m; yes; F; F; F; yes

KEY: (No Census Roll Number given); Name; Date of Birth; Sex; Tribe (Hopi, unless otherwise indicated); Ward [yes or no]; Degree of Father's blood; Degree of Mother's blood; Degree of Child's blood; At jurisdiction where enrolled [yes or no]; (If "no", where?).

ADAMS, Fern; 12-9-1928; f; yes; F; F; F; yes

AHVATZHOIVA, Parlee; 1-22-1929; f; yes; F; F; F; yes

CHAKA, Nellie; 11-28-1928; f; yes; F; F; F; yes

CHEEKA, Alfonso; 4-29-1929; m; yes; F; F; F; yes

CHIO, Alfreda; 9-19-1928; f; yes; F; F; F; yes

CHUSHONGYHIVA, Amy; 11-12-1928; f; yes; F; F; F; yes

DASHEE, Irvin; 1-22-1929; m; yes; F; F; F; yes

DAUNGEVA, Sara; 2-5-1929; f; yes; F; F; F; yes

DOUMA, Lindberg; 12-5-1928; m; yes; F; F; F; yes

DUERINGIVAH, Craig; 8-27-1928; m; yes; F; F; F; yes

DUWAKUKU, George, Jr; 4-17-1929; m; yes; F; F; F; yes

GASHWYTEWA, Karl; 6-23-1929; m; yes; F; F; F; yes

HAMANA, Tracy; 9-22-1928; m; yes; F; F; F; yes

HARVEY, Felix; 11-5-1928; m; yes; F; F; F; yes

HOMEWYTEWA, Dell Ferney; 4-5-1929; f; yes; F; F; F; yes

HONANI, Sara; 2-19-1929; f; yes; F; F; F; yes

HONIANI, Perry Joseph; 1-21-1929; m; yes; F; F; F; yes

HOYOWESE, Opla; 9-7-1928; f; yes; F; F; F; yes

HUMA, Anita; 10-7-1928; f; yes; F; F; F; yes

JAMES, Treva Elizabeth; 4-12-1929; f; yes; F; F; F; yes

JAWANHEFTEWA, Lindberg; 2-3-1929; m; yes; F; F; F; yes

JOHNSON, Wilhelmina; 8-21-1929; f; yes; F; F; F; yes

LIVE BIRTHS, (Occurring between July 1, 1928, and June 30, 1929)

KEY: (No Census Roll Number given); Name; Date of Birth; Sex; Tribe (Hopi, unless otherwise indicated); Ward [yes or no]; Degree of Father's blood; Degree of Mother's blood; Degree of Child's blood; At jurisdiction where enrolled [yes or no]; (If "no", where?).

JOSUMPKA, Elizabeth; 5-18-1929; f; yes; F; F; F; yes

KEWAMWYTEWA, Louise; 12-1-1928; f; yes; F; F; F; yes

KEWANVOYOWMA, Gilbert; 4-1-1929; m; yes; F; F; F; yes

KOINVE, Eldridge; 6-16-1929; m; yes; F; F; F; yes

KUYIYESVA, Lola; 9-1-1928; f; yes; F; F; F; yes

LALOWEE, Beth; 2-1-1929; f; yes; F; F; F; yes

LOMAHEFTEWA, Anna; 3-15-1929; f; yes; F; F; F; yes

LOMAYESTEWA, Hillary; 2-2-1929; m; yes; F; F; F; yes

MAKTIMA, Willard; 4-28-1929; m; yes; F; F; F; yes

MANSFIELD, Dora; 1-28-1929; f; yes; F; F; F; yes

NAHE, Clark; 9-16-1928; m; yes; F; F; F; yes

NAHSONHOYA, Thomas; 10-15-1928; m; yes; F; F; F; yes

NAMINGHA, Dextra; 9-7-1928; f; yes; F; F; F; yes

NASAFATIE, Emily; 4-24-1929; f; yes; F; F; F; yes

NASVASHIE, Minnie; 11-7-1928; f; yes; F; F; F; yes

NAVAMSA, Dolores; 1-21-1929; f; yes; F; F; F; yes

OUTAH, Corita; 9-28-1928; f; yes; F; F; F; yes

OUTAH, Lawrence; 4-3-1929; m; yes; F; F; F; yes

POHONA, Roberta; 1-21-1929; f; yes; F; F; F; yes

POHUMA, Charlotte; 12-28-1928; F; yes; F; F; F; yes

POLACCA, Gazella; 8-10-1928; f; yes; F; F; F; yes

POLACCA, Rebeckah; 8-14-1928; f; yes; F; F; F; yes

LIVE BIRTHS, (Occurring between July 1, 1928, and June 30, 1929)

KEY: (No Census Roll Number given); Name; Date of Birth; Sex; Tribe (Hopi, unless otherwise indicated); Ward [yes or no]; Degree of Father's blood; Degree of Mother's blood; Degree of Child's blood; At jurisdiction where enrolled [yes or no]; (If "no", where?).

POLEWYTEWA, Pansy; 5-19-1929; f; yes; F; F; F; yes

POVATEA, J. Schwarz; 3-23-1929; m; yes; F; F; F; yes

POVATEA, Wilhelmina; 10-25-1928; f; yes; F; F; F; yes

POSEYESVA, Raymond; 7-11-1928; m; yes; F; F; F; yes

QAKWANWA, Mary; 11-23-1928; f; yes; F; F; F; yes

SAHME, Lois; 7-27-1928; f; yes; F; F; F; yes

SAHNEYAH, Herman; 5-12-1929; m; yes; F; F; F; yes

SAKEWA, Francis; 6-26-1929l m; yes; F; F; F; yes

SANDERSON, Clarence Gordon; 5-13-1929; m; yes; F; F; F; yes

SATALA, Ruth; 1-28-1929; f; yes; F; F; F; yes

SAYAHMA, Hope; 3-31-1929; f; yes; F; F; F; yes

SEQUI, Vera; 8-2-1928; f; yes; F; F; F; yes

SHELTON, Henry; 2-1-1929; m; yes; F; F; F; yes

SHULACHIVIE, Eleedia; 8-19-1928; f; yes; F; F; F; yes

SHUNKEE, Ramona; 2-16-1929; f; yes; F; F; F; yes

SOSNEWA, Howard; 6-11-1929; m; yes; F; F; F; yes

TALAUMPTEWA, Perry; 9-10-1928; m; yes; F; F; F; yes

TALAYUMPTEWA, Ruby; 11-8-1928; f; yes; F; F; F; yes

TALLAS, Donald; 9-19-1928; m; yes; F; F; F; yes

TAWAHIEOMA, Nancy; 6-18-1929; f; yes; F; F; F; yes

TEWAWINO, Wilford; 1-30-1929; m; yes; F; F; F; yes

TOUHMA, Mary Elizabeth; 2-27-1929; f; yes; F; F; F; yes

LIVE BIRTHS, (Occurring between July 1, 1928, and June 30, 1929)

KEY: (No Census Roll Number given); Name; Date of Birth; Sex; Tribe (Hopi, unless otherwise indicated); Ward [yes or no]; Degree of Father's blood; Degree of Mother's blood; Degree of Child's blood; At jurisdiction where enrolled [yes or no]; (If "no", where?).

WAZRA, Julia; 2-10-1929; f; yes; F; F; F; yes

LIVE BIRTHS, (Occurring between July 1, 1927, and June 30, 1928)

KEY: (No Census Roll Number given); Name; Date of Birth; Sex; Tribe (Hopi, unless otherwise indicated); Ward [yes or no]; Degree of Father's blood; Degree of Mother's blood; Degree of Child's blood; At jurisdiction where enrolled [yes or no]; (If "no", where?).

ADAMS, Earl Anderson; 2-22-1928; m; yes; F; F; F; yes

ADAMS, Louise; 9-9-1927; f; yes; F; F; F; yes

AHMI, Alexander; 2-1-1928; m; yes; F; F; F; yes

ALBERT, Leland; 10-20-1927; m; yes; F; F; F; yes

CHEKUMIS, Burke; 10-1-1927; m; yes; F; F; F; yes

CHOYKOYCHI, Frank; 3-31-1928; m; yes; F; F; F; yes

COOCHYOUMA, Mathais; 6-30-1928; m; yes; F; F; F; yes

COOKA, Constance Beverly; 4-13-1928; f; yes; F; F; F; yes

DOWAHOYA, Thomas Herman; 10-11-1928; m; yes; F; F; F; yes

DUWAHONGOVA, Belva; 3-13-1928; f; yes; F; F; F; yes

FREDRICK, John; 5-20-1928; m; yes; F; F; F; yes

FREDRICK, Marion; 6-17-1928; f; yes; F; F; F; yes

GAHLAH, Phyllis; 9-25-1927; f; yes; F; F; F; yes

HARRIS, Alvin; 12-28-1928; m; yes; F; F; F; yes

HONANI, Dorothy May; 10-11-1927; f; yes; F; F; F; yes

HONANI, Noble Gray; 4-29-1928; m; yes; F; F; F; yes

HOWATO, Nina; 2-8-1928; f; yes; F; F; F; yes

HUMA, Nuvella; 7-4-1927; f; yes; F; F; F; yes

HUMEWOWMA, Hester; 4-10-1928; f; yes; F; F; F; yes

HYEOMA, Bernie Leo; 10-6-1927; m; yes; F; F; F; yes

JAMES, Bessie; 8-8-1927; f; yes; F; F; F; yes

JENKINS, Violet; 10-15-1927; f; yes; F; F; F; yes

LIVE BIRTHS, (Occurring between July 1, 1927, and June 30, 1928)
KEY: (No Census Roll Number given); Name; Date of Birth; Sex; Tribe (Hopi, unless otherwise indicated); Ward [yes or no]; Degree of Father's blood; Degree of Mother's blood; Degree of Child's blood; At jurisdiction where enrolled [yes or no]; (If "no", where?).

KAWQUAHOEWA, Velta; 11-16-1927; f; yes; F; F; F; yes

KEWANVAYOMA, Vernita; 12-1-1928; f; yes; F; F; F; yes

KOOTSWATEWA, Ansel; 8-26-1927; m; yes; F; F; F; yes

KOYIYUMPTEWA, June; 5-10-1928; m-f; yes; F; F; F; yes

KUYIYESVA, John; 8-25-1927; m; yes; F; F; F; yes

LACAPA, Alberta; 4-1-1928; f; yes; F; F; F; yes

LAHPOO, Florence Means; 3-5-1928; f; yes; F; F; F; yes

LANSA. Betty; 9-29-1928; f; yes; F; F; F; yes

LOMAHEPTEWA, Carol; 6-27-1928; m; yes; F; F; F; yes

LOMAHQUAHU, John; 3-29-1928; m; yes; F; F; F; yes

LOMAKEMA, Stetson; 3-25-1928; m; yes; F; F; F; yes

LOMAVITU, Alvin Bruce; 2-25-1928; m; yes; F; F; F; yes

MAHHO, Benjamin; 5-30-1928; m; yes; F; F; F; yes

MAHLE, Chester; 5-24-1928; m; yes; F; F; F; yes

MAHTSWONGNE, Mildred; 11-30-1927; f; yes; F; F; F; yes

MASANIMPTEWA, Maxine; 3-16-1928; f; yes; F; F; F; yes

MASAYANTIWA, Ellen; 6-18-1928; f; yes; F; F; F; yes

MONNONGE, Nettie; 3-31-1928; f; yes; F; F; F; yes

MOOETESA, Gerald; 5-1-1928; m; yes; F; F; F; yes

NAHA, Josephine; 1-10-1928; f; yes; F; F; F; yes

NAHSINGOENIM, Leon; 4-1-1928; m; yes; F; F; F; yes

NAYATEWA, Zora Adams; 1-4-1928; f; yes; F; F; F; yes

LIVE BIRTHS, (Occurring between July 1, 1927, and June 30, 1928)

KEY: (No Census Roll Number given); Name; Date of Birth; Sex; Tribe (Hopi, unless otherwise indicated); Ward [yes or no]; Degree of Father's blood; Degree of Mother's blood; Degree of Child's blood; At jurisdiction where enrolled [yes or no]; (If "no", where?).

NUMKEWA, Ethel; 7-12-1927; f; yes; F; F; F; yes

NUTUMYA, Peter; 4-1-1928; m; yes; F; F; F; yes

OYAPING, Nelson, Jr; 11-2-1927; m; yes; F; F; F; yes

PAVATEA, Percy; 2-18-1928; m; yes; F; F; F; yes

POLACCA, Jaynes; 5-21-1928; m; yes; F; F; F; yes

POLACCA, Leah; 4-4-1928; f; yes; F; F; F; yes

POLEWYTEWA, Helen; 9-2-1927; f; yes; F; F; F; yes

POLILANEMA, Lawrence; 4-28-1928; m; yes; F; F; F; yes

POOYOWMA, Curtis; 6-30-1928; m; yes; F; F; F; yes

PUHUYESVA, Raymond; 5-4-1928; m; yes; F; F; F; yes

QUAMAHONGNEWA, Blanche; 11-16-1927; f; yes; F; F; F; yes

QUAMANEWA, Clara; 3-2-1928; f; yes; F; F; F; yes

QUAMNA, Merrell; 5-2-1928; m; yes; F; F; F; yes

QUIMAYESSIE, Max; 11-10-1927; m; yes; F; F; F; yes

QUIQUA, Herbert; 4-11-1928; m; yes; F; F; F; yes

SAKEVA, Nellie Charlotte; 9-12-1927; f; yes; F; F; F; yes

SAYAHMA, Elaine; 12-7-1927; f; yes; F; F; F; yes

SEKAQUAPTEWA, Emory, Jr; 12-29-1927; m; yes; F; F; F; yes

SEKIYOUMA, Mary; 5-16-1928; f; yes; F; F; F; yes

SEWEUMPTEWA, Velma; 3-26-1928; f; yes; F; F; F; yes

SHUNKEE, William; 9-10-1927; m; yes; F; F; F; yes

SHUPELA, Beth; 12-4-1927; f; yes; F; F; F; yes

LIVE BIRTHS, (Occurring between July 1, 1927, and June 30, 1928)
KEY: (No Census Roll Number given); Name; Date of Birth; Sex; Tribe (Hopi, unless otherwise indicated); Ward [yes or no]; Degree of Father's blood; Degree of Mother's blood; Degree of Child's blood; At jurisdiction where enrolled [yes or no]; (If "no", where?).

SIHESIMA, Madge; 10-5-1927; f; yes; F; F; F; yes

SILAS, Gertrude; 12-13-1927; f; yes; F; F; F; yes

SOCQUESVIA, Donald; 10-7-1927; m; yes; F; F; F; yes

SUETORKA, Edward; 7-9-1927; m; yes; F; F; F; yes

TAHBO, Polacca; 10-12-1927; m; yes; F; F; F; yes

TAKALA, Max; 10-22-1927; m; yes; F; F; F; yes

TALESTEWAH, Nora; 5-16-1928; f; yes; F; F; F; yes

TALAWYEOSA, Pauline; 4-5-1928; f; yes; F; F; F; yes

TALETSTEMAH, Hazel; 6-22-1928; f; yes; F; F; F; yes

TENACKHONGVA, Iberta; 8-2-1927; f; yes; F; F; F; yes

TUBAKINA, Richard; 5-4-1928; m; yes; F; F; F; yes

WISEOMA, Franklin; 4-25-1928; m; yes; F; F; F; yes

WUNGNEWA, Burton; 5-5-1928; m; yes; F; F; F; yes

YAIVA, Alice; 2-1-1928; f; yes; F; F; F; yes

YOUNGNOIUMA, Harriett; 11-10-1927; f; yes; F; F; F; yes

YOYWETEWA, LeRoy; 10-2-1927; m; yes; F; F; F; yes

ZEENA, Marilyn; 5-19-1928; f; yes; F; F; F; yes

LIVE BIRTHS, (Occurring between July 1, 1926, and June 30, 1927)

KEY: (No Census Roll Number given); Name; Date of Birth; Sex; Tribe (Hopi, unless otherwise indicated); Ward [yes or no]; Degree of Father's blood; Degree of Mother's blood; Degree of Child's blood; At jurisdiction where enrolled [yes or no]; (If "no", where?).

ADAMS, Margaret; 10-17-1926; f; yes; F; F; F; yes

AHVATZHOIYA, Frances; 9-12-1926; f; yes; F; F; F; yes

BAKURZA, Minna; 10-9-1926; f; yes; F; F; F; yes

BATALA, Emil; 11-3-1926; m; yes; F; F; F; yes

CHICUEOMA, June; 5-1-1927; f; yes; F; F; F; yes

CHUAHONGYHIVA, Inez; 3-20-1927; f; yes; F; F; F; yes

CHUAHYOUMA, Lola; 6-24-1927; f; yes; F; F; F; yes

COAATA, Maxine Ashton; 7-20-1926; f; yes; F; F; F; yes

COIN, Ellen; 5-10-1927; f; yes; F; F; F; yes

DUERCHE, George Stewart; 7-10-1926; m; yes; F; F; F; yes

DUERINGIVAH, Eunice; 4-15-1927; f; yes; F; F; F; yes

DUWYIENIE, Winston; 2-24-1927; m; yes; F; F; F; yes

GAYHE, Bertha; 12-16-1926; f; yes; F; F; F; yes

GOYA, Elsa; 6-15-1927; f; yes; F; F; F; yes

HARVEY, Gilman; 9-1-1926; m; yes; F; F; F; yes

HAMEWYTEWA, Martha Washington; 2-22-1927; f; yes; F; F; F; yes

HENNEQUAFTEWA, Gertrude; 8-3-1926; f; yes; F; F; F; yes

HONUMPTIE, Mariana; 7-24-1926; f; yes; F; F; F; yes

JAMES, David; 7-11-1926; m; yes; F; F; F; yes

JAMES, Emmett; 4-7-1927; m; yes; F; F; F; yes

JAWANHEFTEWA, Elvin; 9-4-1926; m; yes; F; F; F; yes

JOHNSON, Edith; 5-4-1927; f; yes; F; F; F; yes

LIVE BIRTHS, (Occurring between July 1, 1926, and June 30, 1927)

KEY: (No Census Roll Number given); Name; Date of Birth; Sex; Tribe (Hopi, unless otherwise indicated); Ward [yes or no]; Degree of Father's blood; Degree of Mother's blood; Degree of Child's blood; At jurisdiction where enrolled [yes or no]; (If "no", where?).

JOSEWYTEWA, Chester; 9-1-1926; m; yes; F; F; F; yes

KASHOINEMA, Bernice; 2-2-1927; f; yes; F; F; F; yes

KEWANEOSEE, Alison; 7-31-1926; m; yes; F; F; F; yes

KEWANVEMA, Lucian; 9-12-1926; m; yes; F; F; F; yes

KEWANWYTEWA, Orrin Davis; 8-17-1926; m; yes; F; F; F; yes

KOOYAQUAPTEWA, Coolidge; 6-2-1927; m; yes; F; F; F; yes

KOYAHONGOVA, Amy; 9-21-1926; f; yes; F; F; F; yes

KOYAHOSOMA, August; 8-9-1926; m; yes; F; F; F; yes

LOMAHEFTEWA, Harvey; 7-4-1926; m; yes; F; F; F; yes

LOMAYESVA, Bernice Elder; 10-5-1926; f; yes; F; F; F; yes

MAHLE, Merle; 7-30-1926; m; yes; F; F; F; yes

MAHAPE, Henry; 5-29-1927; m; yes; F; F; F; yes

MAHTOWONGNE, Horace; 8-4-1926; m; yes; F; F; F; yes

MARKS, Flora; 3-18-1927; f; yes; F; F; F; yes

MASAYANTIWA, Ruth Edson; 9-5-1926; f; yes; F; F; F; yes

MASAYESVA, Mildred; 9-20-1926; f; yes; F; F; F; yes

MASKEEF, Catherine Lull; 3-15-1927; f; yes; F; F; F; yes

MATSWA, Minerva; 1-3-1927; f; yes; F; F; F; yes

MOCKTA, Grant; 2-20-1927; m; yes; F; F; F; yes

MONNONGE, Mabel; 12-31-1926; f; yes; F; F; F; yes

MOOETEWA, Oscar K; 9-14-1926; m; yes; F; F; F; yes

NAHE, Opal; 5-27-1927; f; yes; F; F; F; yes

KEY: (No Census Roll Number given); Name; Date of Birth; Sex; Tribe (Hopi, unless otherwise indicated); Ward [yes or no]; Degree of Father's blood; Degree of Mother's blood; Degree of Child's blood; At jurisdiction where enrolled [yes or no]; (If "no", where?).

NAHPWASIE, (Blank); 8-?-1926; f; yes; F; F; F; yes

NAHSONHOYA, Julius; 11-27-1926; m; yes; F; F; F; yes

NAHVAHSIE, Keith; 7-20-1926; m; yes; F; F; F; yes

NAMINGAH, Warren; 11-10-1926; m; yes; F; F; F; yes

NAMINGHA, Ruth; 11-6-1926; f; yes; F; F; F; yes

NAVAKLOOMA, Lena; 6-17-1927; f; yes; F; F; F; yes

NAVAKUKU; Marietta; 9-21-1926; f; yes; F; F; F; yes

NEVAYKTEWA, James, Jr; 2-4-1927; m; yes; F; F; F; yes

NEVOUNGIATEWA, Lorainne; 5-3-1927; f; yes; F; F; F; yes

NIPHI, Henrietta; 4-22-1927; f; yes; F; F; F; yes

NUTUMYA, John; 8-8-1926; m; yes; F; F; F; yes

NUVAMSA, Susie Charlotte; 6-21-1927; f; yes; F; F; F; yes

OUTAH, Julian Ulysses; 12-8-1926; m; yes; F; F; F; yes

OUTAH, Olive Harriett; 12-8-1926; f; yes; F; F; F; yes

OUTAH, (Blank); 11-10-1926; m; yes; F; F; F; yes

OHKOWYA, Billingsly; 2-9-1927; m; yes; F; F; F; yes

PENTEWA, Dick; 4-12-1927; m; yes; F; F; F; yes

POHHONA, Anna; 4-10-1927; f; yes; F; F; F; yes

POHUMA, Merritt; 5-29-1927; m; yes; F; F; F; yes

POLACCA, Alfred La Fond; 4-14-1927; m; yes; F; F; F; yes

POLACCA, Bernard; 1-20-1927; m; yes; F; F; F; yes

POLEWYTEWA, Harriett; 8-9-1926; f; yes; F; F; F; yes

LIVE BIRTHS, (Occurring between July 1, 1926, and June 30, 1927)
KEY: (No Census Roll Number given); Name; Date of Birth; Sex; Tribe (Hopi, unless otherwise indicated); Ward [yes or no]; Degree of Father's blood; Degree of Mother's blood; Degree of Child's blood; At jurisdiction where enrolled [yes or no]; (If "no", where?).

POLINGUOWMA, Bert; 11-9-1926; m; yes; F; F; F; yes

POLYESTEWA, Katherine; 2-18-1927; f; yes; F; F; F; yes

POVATAH, Jefferson; 1-20-1927; m; yes; F; F; F; yes

POVATEA, Robert Lee; 12-16-1926; m; yes; F; F; F; yes

QAKWANA, John; 12-24-1926; m; yes; F; F; F; yes

QUAHONGEVA, Priscilla; 8-8-1926; f; yes; F; F; F; yes

QUANIMPTEWA, Lester, Jr; 3-23-1927; m; yes; F; F; F; yes

QUOCHITEWA, May Murray; 3-10-1927; f; yes; F; F; F; yes

QUOMAHWAHU, Bertha Rose; 3-1-1927; f; yes; F; F; F; yes

SAHNEYAH, Paul Starring; 10-8-1926; m; yes; F; F; F; yes

SAHU, David; 11-7-1926; m; yes; F; F; F; yes

SANDERSON, Edgar Miller; 6-3-1927; m; yes; F; F; F; yes

SATALA, Alice; 5-7-1927; f; yes; F; F; F; yes

SEECHOMA, Luther; 8-24-1926; m; yes; F; F; F; yes

SEEQUAPTEWA, Lena; 10-24-1926; f; yes; F; F; F; yes

SEEUKTEOMA, Iris; 6-2-1927; f; yes; F; F; F; yes

SEKATAYOU, Clarence; 4-4-1927; m; yes; F; F; F; yes

SEKAYIMPTEWA, Roberta; 2-25-1927; f; yes; F; F; F; yes

SEYOWMA, Doyle Scott; 4-9-1927; m; yes; F; F; F; yes

SHELTON, Peter; 6-4-1927; m; yes; F; F; F; yes

SILAS, Pauline; 6-2-1927; f; yes; F; F; F; yes

SOANEWA, Susie Charlotte; 6-16-1927; f; yes; F; F; F; yes

118

LIVE BIRTHS, (Occurring between July 1, 1926, and June 30, 1927)

KEY: (No Census Roll Number given); Name; Date of Birth; Sex; Tribe (Hopi, unless otherwise indicated); Ward [yes or no]; Degree of Father's blood; Degree of Mother's blood; Degree of Child's blood; At jurisdiction where enrolled [yes or no]; (If "no", where?).

SOUFKIMA, Elbert; 1-17-1927; m; yes; F; F; F; yes

TAHLAHATAMAH, Jewel; 12-10-1926; f; yes; F; F; F; yes

TALANGOYOWNIM, Elinor; 8-7-1926; f; yes; F; F; F; yes

TALAUMPTEWA, Wiley; 10-16-1926; m; yes; F; F; F; yes

TEEMUE, Gilbert; 10-25-1926; m; yes; F; F; F; yes

TUWATSIE, Nettie; 12-18-1926; f; yes; F; F; F; yes

TYMA, Lester; 1-22-1927; m; yes; F; F; F; yes

WAZRA, Dalton; 9-19-1926; m; yes; F; F; F; yes

YOYOWYTEWA, Marion; 5-10-1927; f; yes; F; F; F; yes

ZOAHROKTEIOMA, Ethel; 1-21-1927; f; yes; F; F; F; yes

ZEENA, James; 5-10-1927; m; yes; F; F; F; yes

[No Name]; 7-21-1926; m; yes; F; F; F; yes   Child of Robert Palaala

[No Name]; 7-24-1926; f; yes; F; F; F; yes
                                        Child of Edward Coochwytewa

[No Name]; 7-26-1926; f; yes; F; F; F; yes   Child of Joab Peshpkteoma

[No Name]; 12-25-1926; f; yes; F; F; F; yes   Child of George Bakyoya

LIVE BIRTHS, (Occurring between July 1, 1925, and June 30, 1926)

KEY: (No Census Roll Number given); Name; Date of Birth; Sex; Tribe (Hopi, unless otherwise indicated); Ward [yes or no]; Degree of Father's blood; Degree of Mother's blood; Degree of Child's blood; At jurisdiction where enrolled [yes or no]; (If "no", where?).

ADAMS, Byron; 2-12-1926; m; yes; F; F; F; yes

CHUYOU, Elbert; 6-6-1926; m; yes; F; F; F; yes

COOCHYOUAMA, Sanford; 3-14-1926; m; yes; F; F; F; yes

DASHEE, Stanley, Jr; 6-19-1926; m; yes; F; F; F; yes

DAUNGEVA, Corabel; 2-5-1926; f; yes; F; F; F; yes

DOWAHOYA, Eda; 3-4-1926; f; yes; F; F; F; yes

HOMANA, Virginia; 5-13-1926; f; yes; F; F; F; yes

HOYOWESA, Flora; 5-31-1926; f; yes; F; F; F; yes

HUMA, Norah; 3-23-1926; f; yes; F; F; F; yes

HUMEYOWMA, Lawrence; 6-14-1926; m; yes; F; F; F; yes

KORUH, Erland; 4-18-1926; m; yes; F; F; F; yes

LANSA, May; 4-30-1926; f; yes; F; F; F; yes

LOMAHEPTEWA, Herman; 4-30-1926; m; yes; F; F; F; yes

MAHAPE, Grant; 5-19-1926; m; yes; F; F; F; yes

MAHHO, Bertram Kirschke; 4-9-1926; m; yes; F; F; F; yes

MASANIMPTEWA, Grant; 6-24-1926; m; yes; F; F; F; yes

MASAYESVA, Florence; 6-28-1926; f; yes; F; F; F; yes

MORAN, Lawrence; 4-2-1926; m; yes; F; F; F; yes

ONSAE, Sheila; 6-28-1926; f; yes; F; F; F; yes

OYAPING, Brita; 6-15-1926; f; yes; F; F; F; yes

POACHELE, Raleigh; 2-20-1926; m; yes; F; F; F; yes

POHUMA, Martha Claudia; 5-5-1926; f; yes; F; F; F; yes

LIVE BIRTHS, (Occurring between July 1, 1925, and June 30, 1926)
KEY: (No Census Roll Number given); Name; Date of Birth; Sex; Tribe (Hopi, unless otherwise indicated); Ward [yes or no]; Degree of Father's blood; Degree of Mother's blood; Degree of Child's blood; At jurisdiction where enrolled [yes or no]; (If "no", where?).

POLACCA, Alva; 2-20-1926; f; yes; F; F; F; yes

POLILANEMA, Walter E; 2-7-1926; m; yes; F; F; F; yes

POOLA, Virgil; 5-7-1926; m; yes; F; F; F; yes

POOSHOME, Henley; 5-7-1926; m; yes; F; F; F; yes

POVONTEMA, Luella; 6-26-1926; f; yes; F; F; F; yes

PUHUYESVA, Eloise; 5-8-1926; f; yes; F; F; F; yes

QUIQUA, Judson; 5-7-1926; m; yes; F; F; F; yes

SEEZRO, Lenhart; 5-1-1926; m; yes; F; F; F; yes

SEIMATEWA, Frank; 11-?-1925; m; yes; F; F; F; yes

SEQUAFTEWA, Joe Antoinia; 6-9-1926; m; yes; F; F; F; yes

SEQUI, Melvina; 4-5-1926; f; yes; F; F; F; yes

SHULACHIOVIE, Theodore; 6-23-1926; m; yes; F; F; F; yes

SOSNEWA, Bertha; 6-11-1926; f; yes; F; F; F; yes

SOSSIE, Laverne; 5-14-1926; f; yes; F; F; F; yes

TAHBO, Lorenzo; 2-19-1926; m; yes; F; F; F; yes

TAKALA, Margaret; 5-10-1926; f; yes; F; F; F; yes

TALAALOVENUM, Marietta; 2-3-1926; f; yes; F; F; F; yes

TALAYUMPTEWA, Mawe; 4-12-1926; m; yes; F; F; F; yes

TALAYUMPTEWA, Martin; 3-17-1926; m; yes; F; F; F; yes

TALIS, Pearl; 3-22-1926; f; yes; F; F; F; yes

TAWAHONGNEWA, Grace; 6-25-1926; f; yes; F; F; F; yes

TAWAWINE. Elfrieda; 3-29-1926; f; yes; F; F; F; yes

LIVE BIRTHS, (Occurring between July 1, 1925, and June 30, 1926)

KEY: (No Census Roll Number given); Name; Date of Birth; Sex; Tribe (Hopi, unless otherwise indicated); Ward [yes or no]; Degree of Father's blood; Degree of Mother's blood; Degree of Child's blood; At jurisdiction where enrolled [yes or no]; (If "no", where?).

TOUHMA, Jenness; 4-26-1926; f; yes; F; F; F; yes

TUBAKIMA, Arnold; 4-26-1926; m; yes; F; F; F; yes

YOUNGNOIUMA, Howard; 4-14-1926; m; yes; F; F; F; yes

[No Name]; 5-1-1926; f; yes; F; F; F; yes   Child of Kitty Kemongvisie

DEATHS

of the

HOPI TRIBE

Hopi Indian Agency

Keams Canon,

Arizona 1925 - 1931

KEY: Year; and Number on Last Census Roll (if given); Name; Date of Death; Age at Death; Sex; Tribe (Hopi, unless otherwise indicated); Ward [yes or no]; Degree of Blood; Cause of Death; At jurisdiction where enrolled [yes or no]; (If "no", where?).

BAKURSA, Zella; 3-10-1931; 7 mo; f; yes; F; Measles; yes

1930   7; BONEY, Lotitia Mae; 7-13-1930; 10 yr; f; yes; F; Spinal meningitis; yes

CHACA, Joseph; 10-19-1930; 4 mo; m; yes; F; TB of lungs; yes

1930   26; CHAKA, Lucy Tagie; 12-14-1930; 20 yr; f; yes; F; TB of lungs, yes

1930   29; CHONGWORTHY, Harriet; 3-4-1930; 71 yr; f; yes; F; CA of stomach; yes

COOCHONEVA, *(Blank)*; 1-26-1931; 84 yr; m; yes; F; Myocarditis; yes

HONHONGAVA, Stephen; 2-17-1931; 1 yr; m; yes; F; Malnutrition; yes

HOWATO, Raymond Charles; 1-30-1931; 8 d: m; yes; F; Asphyxia; yes

KACHMANNA, Cleo; 3-30-1931; 1 yr; f; yes; F; Flu; yes

KOINVE, Samuel; 12-23-1930; 4 mo; m; yes; F; Lobar pneumonia

KORUH, Amy; 1-25-1931; 9 mo; f; yes; F; Bronchial pneumonia; yes

1930 101; KORUH, Mary; 10-5-1930; 23 yr; f; yes; F; Pulmonary TB; yes

1930 147; LOMALTESTEWA, *(Blank)*; 9-15-1930; 89 yr; m; yes; F; Acute indigestion; yes

1930 136; LOMATUNA, *(Blank)*; 11-2-1930; 78 yr; m; yes; F; Myocarditis; yes

1930 123; OHKOWYA, Lydia; 10-13-1930; 2 yr; f; yes; F; Malnutrition; yes

OUTAH, Elson; 1-21-1931; 7 mo; m; yes; F; Pneumonia; yes

1930 127; OYAPING, Judith Anna; 3-2-1931; 11 mo; f; yes; F; Measles; yes

PENTEWA, Angelica; 12-10-1930; 11 mo; f; yes; F; TB of meninges; yes

1929 266; PENTEWA, Lorene; 9-4-1930; 8 yr; f; yes; F; Pulmonary TB; yes

1929 264; PENTEWA, Vivian; 8-1-1930; 16 yr; f; yes; F; TB of lungs; yes

1930 192; POLACCA, Leona; 7-6-1930; 30 yr; f; yes; F; TB of lungs; yes

POSEYESVA, Charles; 1-8-1931; 1 yr; m; F; Broncho pneumonia; yes

DEATHS, (Occurring between April 1, 1930, and March 31, 1931)

KEY: Year; and Number on Last Census Roll (if given); Name; Date of Death; Age at Death; Sex; Tribe (Hopi, unless otherwise indicated); Ward [yes or no]; Degree of Blood; Cause of Death; At jurisdiction where enrolled [yes or no]; (If "no", where?).

QUAYELLA, Willie; 11-26-1930; 45 yr; m; F; Acute arthritis; yes

1930   195; SAKAVENKA, Ruth; 11-18-1930; 47 yr; f; yes; F; Nephritis; yes

SAYAHMA, Gerald Moyer; 1-21-1931; 11 d; m; yes; F; Broncho pneumonia; yes

1930   179; SEKATAYOU, Alida; 9-14-1930; 25 yr; f; yes; F; Uterine hemorrhage; yes

SEMEHOYA, Erma; 3-25-1931; 10 mo; f; yes; F; Influenza; yes

1930   251; SHUPELA, Harry; 2-25-1931; 52 yr; m; yes; F; Acute enteritis; yes

1930   293; SUTTA, Mrs. Sake; 2-8-1930; 55 yrs; f; yes; F; Lobar pneumonia; yes

1930   301; TAKALA, Daniel; 3-31-1931; 12 yr; m; yes; F; Pulmonary TB; yes

TAKALA, Owen; 8-26-1930; 1 yr; m; yes; F; Dysentery; yes

TALAYUMPTEWA, Ruby; 8-20-1930; 1 yr; f; yes; F; Dysentery; yes

TEEMA, Tilman; 12-29-1930; 27 d; m; yes; F; Malnutrition; yes

TEEMA, Travis; 12-15-1930; m; yes; F; Malnutrition; yes

1930   30; UMSIE, *(Blank)*; 1-18-1931; 87 yr; f; yes; F; Lobar pneumonia; yes

1930   161; YOUKTI, Harold; 8-13-1930; 40 yr; m; yes; F; Pulmonary TB; yes

1930   300; YOUNGNOIUMA, Lolita; 10-23-1930; 1 yr; f; yes; F; Enteritis; yes

(No name); 11-17-1930; 1 d; f; yes; F; Unknown; yes
Child of Roland Nehoitewa

(No name); 12-20-1930; ?; m; yes; F; Still birth; yes;
Child of Henry Niphi

DEATHS, (Occurring between July 1, 1929, and June 30, 1930)

KEY: Year; and Number on Last Census Roll (if given); Name; Date of Death; Age at Death; Sex; Tribe (Hopi, unless otherwise indicated); Ward [yes or no]; Degree of Blood; Cause of Death; At jurisdiction where enrolled [yes or no]; (If "no", where?).

1929   4; ADAMS, Louise; 2-6-1930; 2 yr; f; yes; F; Moth ball poisoning; yes

1929   26; AHVATZHOIYA, Parlee; 1-17-1930; 11 mo; f; yes; F; Unknown; yes

1929   135; COONYA, *(Blank)*; 3-9-1930; 80 yr; f; yes; F; Senility; yes

    DUAHKPOO, *(Blank)*; 5-28-1930; 79 yr; m; yes; F; Lobar pneumonia; yes

1929   44; HONUMPTIE, Calvin; 10-8-1929; 1yr; m; yes; F; Unknown; yes

    HONWESIMA, Mary Agnes; 5-27-1930; 8 mo; f; yes; F; Pulmonary TB; yes

1929   29; HOOLA, *(Blank)*; 8-9-1929; 71 yr; m; yes; F; Cerebral hemorrhage; yes

    HOWATO, Bennett; 1-26-1930; 2 mo; m; yes; F; Hydrocephalus; yes

    HOWATO, Russell; 11-15-1929; 10 d; m; yes; F; Unknown; yes

1929   70; KEWANEOSEE, Allison; 8-6-1929; 3 yr; m; yes; F; TB of peritoneum; yes

1929   16; KEWANYMN, *(Blank)*; 11-21-1929; 48 yr; f; yes; F; Coronary embolus; yes

1929   110; KOOYAHOONIM, *(Blank)*; 11-20-1929; 72 yr; f; yes; F; Unknown; yes

1929   89; KUUENEMPTEWA, Salabi; 2-12-1930; 46 yr; f; yes; F; Cerebromalacia; yes

    LALOWEE, Beth; 7-1-1929; 5 mo; f; yes; F; Bronchial pneumonia; yes

1929   107; LESSO, *(Blank)*; 5-7-1930; 64 yr; m; yes; F; Lobar pneumonia; yes

    LOMAHEFTEWA, Anna; 8-1-1929; 4 mo; f; yes; F; Cholera infantum; yes

1929   138; MATZWA, Clifford Gordon; 7-1-1929; 5 yr; m; yes; F; TB of lungs; yes

1929   201; MONNONGE, Mabel; 3-29-1930; 3 yr; f; yes; F; Influenza; yes

1929   141; MOOETEWA, Gerald; 8-26-1929; 1yr; m; yes; F; Cholera infantum; yes

1929   209; POVATAH, Jefferson; 2-23-1930; 3 yr; m; yes; F; TB of lungs; yes

1929   111; POOLA, Wave; 6-22-1930; 16 yr; f; yes; F; Pulmonary TB; yes

DEATHS, (Occurring between July 1, 1929, and June 30, 1930)

KEY: Year; and Number on Last Census Roll (if given); Name; Date of Death; Age at Death; Sex; Tribe (Hopi, unless otherwise indicated); Ward [yes or no]; Degree of Blood; Cause of Death; At jurisdiction where enrolled [yes or no]; (If "no", where?).

1929   207;   QUAMAHONGNEVA, Sunbeam; 7-2-1929; 16 yr; f; yes; F; TB of lungs; yes

SANDERSON, Clarence Gordon; 1-23-1930; 8 mo; m; yes; F; Hemorrhagic encephalitis; yes

1929   226;   SEAPHY, Philip; 3-27-1930; 22 yr; m; yes; F; TB of lungs; yes

1929   332;   SEHONGNEWA, *(Blank)*; 4-1-1930; 87 yr; m; yes; F; Unknown; yes

SEHONGVA, Scott; 8-3-1929; 3 mo; m; yes; F; Infected burns; yes

SEKAIBISHE, Rose; 5-4-1930; 8 yr; f; yes; F; Broncho pneumonia; yes

SUETOPKA, Esther; 11-30-1929; 16 d; f; yes; F; Infected sores; yes

TAHLSTATEMAH, Hazel; 2-27-1930; 1 yr; f; yes; F; Cholera infantum; yes

1929   296;   TAKALA, John; 11-19-1929; 14 yr; m; yes; F; Peritonitis, general; yes

1929   208;   TALASYAMSE, Lawerence Moran; 3-6-1930; 3 yr; m; yes; F; Pulmonary TB; yes

TALAYUMPTEWA, Roscoe; 11-20-1929; 10 yr; m; yes; F; Epilepsy; yes

1929   239;   TALAYUMPTEWA, Winnie; 3-26-1930; 23 yr; f; yes; F; Pulmonary TB; yes

1929   276;   TOBY, Caddo; 9-5-1929; 23 yr; m; yes; F; Drowning - accidental; yes

1929   420;   TUVANWYTEMA, *(Blank)*; 7-8-1929; 77 yr; m; yes; F; Unknown; yes

TWOITSIE, Magdelena Rose; 2-6-1930; 4 mo; f; yes; F; Broncho pneumonia; yes

1929   288;   WINNUTAH, John; 2-4-1930; 77 yr; m; yes; F; Senility; yes

YONANI, Hugh; 5-4-1930; 12 yr; m; yes; F; Broncho pneumonia; yes

YOUYUWYYA, Laura Mae; 11-29-1929; 28 d; f; yes; F; Infantile convulsions; yes

KEY: Year; and Number on Last Census Roll (if given); Name; Date of Death; Age at Death; Sex; Tribe (Hopi, unless otherwise indicated); Ward [yes or no]; Degree of Blood; Cause of Death; At jurisdiction where enrolled [yes or no]; (If "no", where?).

BACON, James; 6-4-1929; 53 yr; m; yes; F; TB of lungs; yes

BAKURZA, Minna; 2-3-1929; 2 yr; f; yes; F; Unknown; yes

BATALA, Hunlley; 4-26-1929; 16 yr; m; yes; F; TB of lungs; yes

CAHAYO, *(Blank)*; 1-9-1929; 91 yr; f; yes; F; Lobar pneumonia; yes

CEVENTEWA, *(Blank)*; 1-3-1929; 71 yr; m; yes; F; Senile pneumonia; yes

CHEEH, *(Blank)*; 11-2-1928; 61 yr; f; yes; F; General septicemia; yes

DUERINGIVAH, Alta; 8-27-1928; 33 yr; f; yes; F; Puerperal septicemia; yes

DUERINGIVAH, Craig; 9-21-1928; 24 d; m; yes; F; General septicemia; yes

DUWAHONGVA, Belva; 2-2-1929; 11 m; f; yes; F; Infected impetigo sores; yes

HOKONA, *(Blank)*; 5-20-1929; 54 yr; f; yes; F; Accidental fall from Mesa; yes

HONANI, Nobel Gray; 3-12-1929; 10 m; m; yes; F; Broncho pneumonia; yes

HONANI, Sara; 6-8-1929; 3 m; f; yes; F; Cholera infantum; yes

JAWANHEFTEWA, Lindberg; 2-8-1929; 5 d; m; yes; F; Unknown; yes

JOSWENSIE, Belle; 2-3-1929; 50 yr; f; yes; F; Post-partum hemorrhage; yes

KASHOINEMA, Hubert; 3-6-1929; 6 m; m; yes; F; Broncho pneumonia; yes

KEAQUOOHA, *(Blank)*; 9-8-1928; 74 yr; f; yes; F; Unknown; yes

KEWANEOSEE, Myrna; 3-28-1929; 7yr; f; yes; TB of lungs; yes

KEWANHONEOMA, *(Blank)*; 1-24-1929; 81 yr; m; yes; F; Unknown; yes

DEATHS, (Occurring between July 1, 1928, and June 30, 1929)

KEY: Year; and Number on Last Census Roll (if given); Name; Date of Death; Age at Death; Sex; Tribe (Hopi, unless otherwise indicated); Ward [yes or no]; Degree of Blood; Cause of Death; At jurisdiction where enrolled [yes or no]; (If "no", where?).

KWANVEMA, Jennie; 2-1-1929; 50 yr; f; yes; F; Infected carcinoma of colon; yes

KOYIYUMPTEWA, June; 11-10-1928; 6 m; f; yes; F; Unknown; yes

LACAPA, Sam P; 10-14-1928; 34 yr; m; yes; F; Lobar pneumonia; yes

LOMAYESTEWA, Hillary; 5-29-1929; 3 m; m; yes; F; Broncho pneumonia; yes

LOMAYOYA, Reba; 12-19-1928; 46 yr; f; yes; F; Influenza; yes

MAHAPE, Norris; 1-15-1929; 6 yr; m; yes; F; Nose hemorrhages; yes

MORAN, Asa; 4-23-1929; 18 yr; m; yes; F; Chronic nephritis; yes

POLACCA, Gazella; 11-16-1928; 1 m; f; yes; F; Cholera infantum; yes

POLEYUQUIE, *(Blank)*; 2-6-1929; 61 yr; f; yes; F; Unknown; yes

QUAMAHONGNEWA, Cortney; 2-13-1929; 4 yr; m; yes; F; Unknown; yes

QUONAHQUAPTEWA, Arthur; 11-17-1928; 23 yr; m; yes; F; Unknown; yes

SEENTEWA, Donald; 3-23-1929; 15 yr; m; yes; F; TB of lungs; yes

TAHBO, Dona; 1-3-1929; 34 yr; f; yes; F; Uterine Hemorrhage; yes

TAHLETSTEMAH, *(Blank)*; 1-11-1929; 39 yr; m; yes; F; TB of lungs; yes

TALAGAYOISE, *(Blank)*; 2-3-1929; 101 yr; f; yes; F; Old age; yes

TALASYAMSE, Dollie; 4-3-`919; 35 yr; f; yes; F; TB of lungs; yes

TALAUMPTEWA, Perry; 10-4-1928; 24 d; m; yes; F; Unknown; yes

TUAVHONGOVA, *(Blank)*; 2-21-1929; 68 yr; m; yes; F; Unknown; yes

UYOUNGWA, *(Blank)*; 3-4-1929; ?; m; yes; F; Stillbirth; yes

WAZRA, Julia; 5-8-1929; 2 mo; f; yes; F; Broncho pneumonia; yes

128

DEATHS, (Occurring between July 1, 1928, and June 30, 1929)

KEY: Year; and Number on Last Census Roll (if given); Name; Date of Death; Age at Death; Sex; Tribe (Hopi, unless otherwise indicated); Ward [yes or no]; Degree of Blood; Cause of Death; At jurisdiction where enrolled [yes or no]; (If "no", where?).

YOUKEOMA, *(Blank)*; 2-23-1929; 36 yr; m; yes; Accidental fall; yes

YOUYUWYE, *(Blank)*; 2-12-1929; 81 yr; m; yes; F; TB of lungs; yes

DEATHS, (Occurring between July 1, 1927, and June 30, 1928)

KEY: Year; and Number on Last Census Roll (if given); Name; Date of Death; Age at Death; Sex; Tribe (Hopi, unless otherwise indicated); Ward [yes or no]; Degree of Blood; Cause of Death; At jurisdiction where enrolled [yes or no]; (If "no", where?).

ADAMS, Margaret; 1-9-1928; 1 yr; f; yes; F; Measles; yes

BAKURZA, Minna; 2-9-1928; 4 m; f; yes; F; yes; Pneumonia; yes

CAMAYESTEWA, *(Blank)*; 9-17-1927; 83 yr; m; yes; F; Cardio, renal disease; *(blank)*

CHUAHYOUMA, Lola; 11-9-1927; 4 m; f; yes; F; Unknown; yes

COIN, Ellen; 1-16-1928; 8 m; m; yes; F; Pneumonia; yes

DAUNGEVA, Corabel; 3-19-1928; 2 yr; f; yes; F; Whooping cough; yes

DENEBE, Gloria; 9-16-1927; 2 yr; f; yes; F; Unknown; yes

DUERCHE, George Stewart; 2-24-1928; 1 yr; m; yes; F; Lobar pneumonia, yes

GASHWYTEWA, Ben; 9-1-1927; 2 yr; m; yes; F; Bronchial pneumonia; yes

HONANI, Dolly May; 4-11-1928; 6 m; f; yes; Whooping cough; yes

HONANI, Dorothy May; 12-12-1927; 1 m; f; yes; F; Malnutrition; yes

HONANI, Calvin; 10-27-1927; 1 yr; m; yes; F; Measles; yes

HOYOWESVA, Flora; 8-12-1927; 1 yr; f; yes; F; Bronchial pneumonia; yes

HUMA, Nuvella; 8-14-1927; 1 m; f; yes; F; Unknown; yes

HUMEUOUMA, Lawrence; 4-4-1928; 1 yr; m; yes; F; Broncho-pneumonia; yes

IHOYEA, John; 3-2-1928; 21 yr; m; yes; F; TB of lungs; yes

JAWANHETEWA, Elvin; 1-9-1928; 1 yr; m; yes; F; Pneumonia; yes

JOSEWYTEWA, Chester; 10-6-1927; 1 m; m; yes; F; Measles; yes

KEWANVEYOWMA, Bernita; 4-29-1928; 4 m; F; yes; Whooping cough; yes

DEATHS, (Occurring between July 1, 1927, and June 30, 1928)

KEY: Year; and Number on Last Census Roll (if given); Name; Date of Death; Age at Death; Sex; Tribe (Hopi, unless otherwise indicated); Ward [yes or no]; Degree of Blood; Cause of Death; At jurisdiction where enrolled [yes or no]; (If "no", where?).

KOMAHHEWA, Eli; 12-28-1927; 48 yr; m; yes; F; Pneumonia; yes

KOOYAQUAPTEWA, Coolidge; 3-6-1928; 9 m; m; yes; F; Broncho pneumonia; yes

KOSANO, *(Blank)*; 2-2-1928; 74 yr; m; yes; F; TB of lungs; yes

KUYIYESVA, John; 9-1-1927; 24 d; m; yes; F; Smothered; yes

LACAPA, Venus; 3-3-1928; 2 yr; f; yes; F; Influenza; yes

LAHPOO, Lucas; 3-3-1928; 2 yr; m; yes; F; Broncho pneumonia; yes

LOMACUEVA, *(Blank)*; 7-20-1927; 75 yr; m; yes; F; Old age; yes

LOMAHEPTEWA, Herman; 9-8-1927; 1 yr; m; yes; F; Bronchial pneumonia; yes

LOMAHEPTEWA, Leona; 8-21-1928; 2 yr; f; yes; F; Bronchial pneumonia; yes

LOMAHVEMA, Aline; 3-7-1928; 8yr; f; yes; F; Unknown; yes

LOMASNEWA, Francis; 11-30-1927; 8 yr; f; yes; F; TB; yes

LOMAVENTEWA, *(Blank)*; 8-2-1927; 80 yr; f; yes; F; Old age; yes

MAHAPA, Henry; 5-6-1928; 5 m; m; yes; F; Bronchial pneumonia; yes

MAHLE, Merle; 1-11-1928; 1 yr; m; yes; F; Rickets; yes

MAHTSONGIVE, Mildred Krouch; 3-6-1928; 3 m; f; yes; F; Broncho pneumonia; yes

MASAKWAPTIWA, Gladys; 8-30-1927; 48 yr; f; yes; F; Child birth; yes

MASANIMPTEWA, Grant; 9-7-1928; 1 yr; m; yes; F; Bronchial pneumonia; yes

MASAQUAPTEWA, Marjoria; 6-12-1928; 6 yr; f; yes; F; Pneumonia; yes

MASAYANTIEWA, Ruth Edson; 9-10-1927; 1 yr; f; yes; F; Unknown; yes

MASAYESVA, Florence; 3-13-1928; 1 yr; f; yes; F; Whooping cough; yes

131

DEATHS, (Occurring between July 1, 1927, and June 30, 1928)

KEY: Year; and Number on Last Census Roll (if given); Name; Date of Death; Age at Death; Sex; Tribe (Hopi, unless otherwise indicated); Ward [yes or no]; Degree of Blood; Cause of Death; At jurisdiction where enrolled [yes or no]; (If "no", where?).

MATZWA, Minerva; 4-24-1928; 1 yr; f; yes; F; Acute peritonis[sic]; yes

MOOTETWA, Faith; 3-11-1928; 3 yr; f; yes; F; Broncho pneumonia; yes

MORNAH, *(Blank)*; 11-17-1927; 81yr; m; yes; F; Broken neck; yes

NAHWASIE, Keith; 3-5-1928; 1 yr; m; yes; F; Broncho pneumonia; yes

NAMINGAH, Donald; 9-6-1927; 2 yr; m; yes; F; Bronchial pneumonia; yes

NAVAOYESVA, Mack; 4-6-1928; 17yr; m; yes; F; TB of lungs; yes

NAVAMSA, Susie Charlott; 12-8-1927; 5 m; f; yes; F; Unknown; yes

NAVAMSA, Virginia; 1-26-1928; 4 yr; f; yes; F; Cerebrospinal fever; yes

NAYATEWA, Zora Adams; 4-28-1928; 3 m; f; yes; F; Whooping cough; yes

NEVAYKTEWA, Fanny; 9-21-1927; 2 yr; f; yes; F; Measles; yes

NUMKEWA, Elden; 10-6-1927; 2 yr; m; yes; F; Pneumonia; yes

NUTUMYA, John; 8-25-1927; 2 m; m; yes; F; Bronchial pneumonia; yes

NUTUMYA, Peter; 8-23-1927; 2 yr; m; yes; F; Bronchial pneumonia; yes

OHKOWYA, Billingsley; 10-9-1927; 8 m; m; yes; F; Measles; yes

OUTAH, Julian Ulysses; 10-7-1927; 10 m; m; yes; F; Measles; yes

OYAPING, Nelson, Jr; 11-11-1927; 9 d; m; yes; F; Unknown; yes

PECUSA, Aaron; 9-29-1927; 24 yr; m; yes; F; Pulmonary TB; yes

PESHOKTEOMA, Fern; 11-20-1927; 27 yr; f; yes; F; Infection childbirth; yes

POHHOMA, Anna; 3-28-1928; 11 m; f; yes; F; Broncho pneumonia; yes

POHUMA, Merritt; 8-24-1927; 1 m; m; yes; F; Unknown; yes

POLEYESVA, *(Blank)*; 10-19-1927; 54 yr; m; yes; F; Unknown; yes

POOLA, Virginia; 3-9-1928; 1 yr; f; yes; F; Broncho pneumonia; yes

POONYAHWEMKA, *(Blank)*; 1-3-1928; 79 yr; f; yes; F; Influenza; yes

POOSHOME, Henley; 5-5-1928; 1 yr; m; yes; F; Lobar pneumonia; yes

POOYOWMA, Murial; 8-24-1927; 2 yr; f; yes; F; Bronchial pneumonia; yes

PUHUYESVA, Eloise; 5-2-1928; 2 yr; f; yes; F; Inanition; yes

QUANNO, Thelma Ruth; 5-1-1928; 4 yr; f; yes; F; Strychnine poison; yes

QUAMAHONGNEWA, Blanche; 4-18-1928 5 m; f; yes; F; Whooping cough; yes

QUANIMPTEWA, Lester, Jr; 9-15-1927; 6 m; m; yes; F; Double lobar pneumonia; yes

QUANIMPTEWA, Martha Joan; 10-6-1927; 2 yr; f; yes; F; Measles; yes

QUEIVIE, Zettie; 11-19-1927; 40 yr; f; yes; F; Unknown; yes

QNACHITEWA[sic], May Murray; 1-3-1928; 9 m; f; yes; F; Unknown; yes

SAHNEYAH, Lorain Delight; 3-15-1928; 3 yr; f; yes; F; Broncho pneumonia; yes

SATALA, Alice; 3-12-1928; 10 m; f;yes; F; Broncho pneumonia; yes

SEECHOMA, Luther; 43-4-1928; 1 yr; m; yes; F; Broncho pneumonia; yes

SEEQUAPTEWA, Lena; 8-31-1927; 10 m; f; yes; F; Broncho pneumonia; yes

SEEZRO, Lenhart; 10-17-1927; 5m m; yes; F; Measlea[sic]; yes

SEKIYOWMA, Mary; 5-12-1928; 23 d; f; yes; F; Abscesses; yes

SEWAQUABE, *(Blank)*; 12-17-1927; 81 yr; f; yes; F; Senility; yes

SHULACHIVIE, Theodore; 2-29-1928; 1 yr; m; yes; F; Broncho pneumonia; yes

DEATHS, (Occurring between July 1, 1927, and June 30, 1928)

KEY: Year; and Number on Last Census Roll (if given); Name; Date of Death; Age at Death; Sex; Tribe (Hopi, unless otherwise indicated); Ward [yes or no]; Degree of Blood; Cause of Death; At jurisdiction where enrolled [yes or no]; (If "no", where?).

SHUNKEE, William; 2-12-1928; 5 m; m; yes; F; Broncho pneumonia; yes

SOQUEVIA, Donald; 5-25-1928; 8 m; m; yes; F; Bronchial pneumonia; yes

SOUFKIMA, Elbert; 4-22-1928; 3 m; m; yes; F; Whooping cough; yes

TAHBO, Polacca; 3-9-1928; 4 m; m; yes; F; Broncho pneumonia; yes

TAHLETSTEMAH, Jewel; 1-2-1928; 1 yr; f; yes; F; Measles; yes

TALANGAYOWNIM, Elinor; 7-25-1927; 11 m; f; yes; F; Inanition; yes

TALASNIMPTEWA, *(Blank)*; 11-13-1927; 85 yr; m; yes; F; Valvular heart disease; yes

TALAUMPTEWA, Wiley; 10-1-1927; 11 m; m; yes; F; Unknown; yes

TULAWISUMA, *(Blank)*; 2-28-1928; 62 yr; m; yes; F; Influenza; yes

TALESTEMAH, Jean; 5-4-1928; 9 yr; m; yes; F; TB of lungs; yes

TALUMPTEWA, Lettie; 6-23-1928; 3 yr; f; yes; F; Cerebral meningitis; yes

TAWAHONGNEWA, Maxine; 8-17-1927; 1 yr; f; yes; F; Bronchial pneumonia; yes

TEWAMANEWA, Wilson; 1-31-1928; 21 yr; m; yes; F; Accidental injury; yes

TUBAKINA, Arnold; 2-23-1928; 1 yr; m; yes; F; Lobar pneumonia; yes

TUWATSIE, Nettie; 5-5-1928; 1 yr; f; yes; F; Broncho pneumonia; yes

TYMA, Lester; 10-23-1927; 9 m; m; yes; F; Measles; yes

WAYRA, Harry; 9-19-1927; 20 yr; m; yes; F; TB; yes

WISEOMA, Theodore; 7-11-1927; 11 yr; m; yes; F; Tubercular meningitis; yes

WOOPAH, *(Blank)*; 9-23-1927; 95 yr; m; yes; F; Unknown; yes

134

DEATHS, (Occurring between July 1, 1927, and June 30, 1928)

KEY: Year; and Number on Last Census Roll (if given); Name; Date of Death; Age at Death; Sex; Tribe (Hopi, unless otherwise indicated); Ward [yes or no]; Degree of Blood; Cause of Death; At jurisdiction where enrolled [yes or no]; (If "no", where?).

YOUNGNOIUMA, Howard; 7-22-1927; 1 yr; m; yes; F; Unknown; yes

YOYETEWA, LeRoy; 2-2-1928; 4 m; m; yes; F; Unknown; yes

YOYOKE, Cleve; 6-10-1928; 21 yr; m; yes; F; Accidental fall; yes

YOYOWAYTIWA, Marian; 4-25-1928; 11 m; f; yes; F; Unknown; yes

ZOSHROKTEIOMA, Ethel; 11-3-1927; 11 m; f; yes; F; Measles; yes

[Unnamed]; 8-31-1927; 1 da; m; yes; F; Unknown; yes
Child of Frank Masakwaptiwa

** [Unnamed]; 12-1-1927; 19 d; m; yes; F; Injured during birth; yes
Child of Joab Peshokteoma

** *(No name)*; 12-1-1927; ?; m; yes; F; Stillbirth; yes
Child of Joab Peshokteoma

*(**NOTE: Probably same child listed both ways.)*

(No name); 10-28-1927; ?; m; yes; F; Stillbirth; yes
Child of Perry Kewnvema

(No name); 1-6-1928; ?; m; yes; F; Stillbirth; yes
Child of Henry Oyoungwa

KEY: Year; and Number on Last Census Roll (if given); Name; Date of Death; Age at Death; Sex; Tribe (Hopi, unless otherwise indicated); Ward [yes or no]; Degree of Blood; Cause of Death; At jurisdiction where enrolled [yes or no]; (If "no", where?).

BACOSMA, Jack; 5-11-1927; 13 yr; m; yes; F; TB; yes

CHUYOU, Elbert; 8-10-1926; 2 m; m; yes; F; Lobar pneumonia; yes

COIN, Caroline; 7-12-1926; 10 m; f; yes; F; Membranous croup; yes

DENEBE, Alice; 4-13-1927; 18 yr; f; yes; F; Unknown; yes

GREELEY, Horace; 8-17-1926; 90 yr; m; yes; F; Senility; yes

HONUMPTIE, Marianna; 9-28-1926; 2 m; f; yes; F; Malnutrition; yes

HUMA, Norah; 8-22-1926; 5 m; f; yes; F; Lobar pneumonia; yes

HUNTER, Allen; 7-17-1926; 50 yr; m; yes; F; TB of lungs; yes

JAMES, David; 9-4-1926; 1 m; m; yes; F; Unknown; yes

KOMAQUAPTEWA, Sam; 5-1-1926; 45 yr; m; yes; F; Found dead; yes

KOMAYAMTEWA, *(Blank)*; 7-6-1926; 69 yr; m; yes; F; Double pneumonia; yes

KOYAHOEOMA, Lucille; 2-28-1927; 3 yr; f; yes; F; Pneumonia; yes

KOYAHONGOVA, Amy; 12-23-1926; 3 m; f; yes; F; Unknown; yes

KOWANOIYA, *(Blank)*; 8-26-1926; 95 yr; f; yes; F; Accidental fall from roof; yes

KUYIYESVA, Ethan; 5-6-1927; 5 yr; m; yes; F; Bronchial pneumonia; yes

LESSO, Luella; 7-26-1926; 1 yr; F; yes; F; Cholera sefantum; no; P.O. Phoenix, AZ

LOMAHQUAHU, Harry; 8-11-1926; 1 yr; m; yes; F; Marasmus; yes

LOMANYESTEWA, *(Blank)*; 3-22-1927; 84 yr; m; yes; F; Influenza; yes

LOMASNEWA, Henry; 3-19-1927; 50 yr; m; yes; F; Pneumonia; yes

MAHTSWONGNE, Horace; 9-2-1926; 29 d; m; yes; F; Marasmus; yes

MASAMANEWA, *(Blank)*; 4-24-1927; 80 yr; m; yes; Old age; yes

DEATHS, (Occurring between July 1, 1926, and June 30, 1927)

KEY: Year; and Number on Last Census Roll (if given); Name; Date of Death; Age at Death; Sex; Tribe (Hopi, unless otherwise indicated); Ward [yes or no]; Degree of Blood; Cause of Death; At jurisdiction where enrolled [yes or no]; (If "no", where?).

MASAQUAPTEWA, Amy; 9-16-1926; 11 m; f; yes; F; Marasmus; yes

MOOSTEWA, Oscar; 9-21-1926; 7 d; m; yes; F; Infected naval; yes

NAMINGHA, Ruth; 11-27-1926; 21 d; f; yes; F; Pneumonia; yes

NEVATOOTAMANNA, Lila; 7-25-1926; 12 yr; f; yes; F; Influenza; yes

NEVAYKTEWA, James; 2-22-1927; 18 d; m; yes; F; Bowel trouble; yes

NIPHI, Viola; 7-10-1926; 1 yr; f; yes; F; Diarrhea; yes

NUTUMYA, John; 10-20-1926; 2 m; m; yes; Unknown; yes

OYAPING, Brita; 6-25-1927; 1 yr; f; yes; F; TB; yes

PENTEWA, Christine; 12-1-1926; 16yr; f; yes; F; Pulmonary TB; yes

PENTEWA, Myrtle; 11-31-1926; 1 yr; f; yes; F; Ententis[sic]; yes

PESHOKTEOMA, Georgene; 11-22- 1926; 4 m; f; yes; F; Pneumonia; yes

POACHELE, Raliegh; 4-6-1927; 1 yr; m; yes; F; Bronchial pneumonia; yes

POHUMA, Martha Claudia; 7-12-1926; 2 m; f; yes; F; Cholera infan tum; yes

POLACCA, Alfred LaFond; 4-26-1927; 12 d; m; yes; F; Inanition; yes

POLACCA, Bernard; 3-15-1927; 1 m; m; yes; F; Enteritis; yes

POLINGYOWMA, Lizzie; 5-27-1927; 22 yr; f; yes; F; Pulmonary TB; yes

POOSHOME, Leila; 3-3-1927; 8 yr; f; yes; F; Pneumonia; yes

QUAHONGAVA, Priscilla; 5-12-1927; 9 m; f; yes; F; Bowel trouble; yes

SAKQUESVA, Gertrude; 8-12-1926; f; yes; F; Marasmus; yes

SAKATAYOU, Clarence; 4-10-1927; 7 d; m; yes; F; Bowel trouble; yes

SILAS, Gretchen; 10-10-1926; 1 yr; f; yes; F; Cholera infantum; yes

SUWANYA, *(Blank)*; 1-1-1927; 76 yr; m; yes; F; Unknown; yes

137

DEATHS, (Occurring between July 1, 1926, and June 30, 1927)
KEY: Year; and Number on Last Census Roll (if given); Name; Date of Death; Age at Death; Sex; Tribe (Hopi, unless otherwise indicated); Ward [yes or no]; Degree of Blood; Cause of Death; At jurisdiction where enrolled [yes or no]; (If "no", where?).

TAHBO, Ramon; 7-26-1926; 10 yr; m; yes; F; Acute Bright's disease; yes

TAKALA; Margaret; 5-3-1927; 11 m; f; yes; F; Bronchial pneumonia; yes

TALASHONEMA, *(Blank)*; 5-13-1927; 54 yr; f; yes; F; Unknown; yes

TATECKINVE, Douglas; 3-18-1927; 16 yr; m; yes; F; Lobar pneumonia; yes

VENTEWA, Alberta; 4-12-1927; 12 yr; f; yes; F; Pulmonary TB; yes

WICKAYAM, *(Blank)*; 8-23-1926; 87 yr; m; yes; F; Bronchitis; yes

WISEOMA, Wayne; 7-6-1926; 6 yr; m; yes; F; Fractured skull; yes

ZEENA, James; 6-12-1927; 1 m; m; yes; F; Unknown; yes

ZEENA, Rosita; 7-23-1926; 1 yr; f; yes; F; Cholera infantum; yes

(No name); 7-23-1926; 2 d; m; yes; F; Pre-natal; yes
                                        Child of Rober[sic] Palaala

(No name); 7-30-1926; 6 d; f; yes; F; Malnutrition; yes
                                        Child of Edward Coochwytewa

POVATIA, Tom; 7-22-1926; ?; m; yes; F; Stillborn; yes

SHUPELA, *(Blank)*; 10-24-1926; ?; m; yes; F; Stillborn; yes

DEATHS, (Occurring between July 1, 1925, and June 30, 1926)
KEY: Year; and Number on Last Census Roll (if given); Name; Date of Death; Age at Death; Sex; Tribe (Hopi, unless otherwise indicated); Ward [yes or no]; Degree of Blood; Cause of Death; At jurisdiction where enrolled [yes or no]; (If "no", where?).

BASHING, Lee, Jr; 2-7-1926; 1 yr; m; yes; F; Heart failure; yes

CHUAHONGYHIVA, Evert; 2-7-1926; 1 m; m; yes; F; Unknown; yes

COIN, Harold; 2-23-1926; 2 yr; m; yes; F; Empyema; yes

CONGEYAH, *(Blank)*; 5-2-1926; 69 yr; m; yes; F; Pulmonary TB; yes

DEWAHOYA, Eda; 3-22-1926; 18 d; f; yes; F; Malnutrition; yes

HOWATA, Peter; 2-22-1926; 13 yr; m; yes; F; Pulmonary TB; yes

JOHNSON (Kuwanyisnom), Nellie; 2-23-1926; 46 yr; f; yes; F; Contusion of the brain; yes

KEWANHOUGKA, Joyce; 4-1-1926; 60 yr; f; yes; F; Spinal meningitis; yes

LOMAHWYMA, Dollie; 2-24-1926; 1 m; f; yes; F; Unknown; yes

MACHVUH, William; 5-19-1926; 33 yr; m; yes; F; Pulmonary TB; yes

MAHAPE, Grant; 6-7-1926; 19 d; m; yes; F; Unknown; yes

NAVAKLEOMA, Louise; 6-21-1926; 1 yr; f; yes; F; Diarrhea; yes

PIKI, Pika; 6-29-1926; 79 yr; f; yes; F; Old age; yes

POLEWHOEMA, Lottie; 2-23-1926; 1 yr; f; yes; F; Influenza; yes

POLEWYMA (Polewisnim), May; 2-22-1926; 30 yr; f; yes; F; Influenza; yes

PONCHO, Laura; 4-21-1926; 4 m; f; yes; F; Prenatal malnutrition; yes

POVATAH, Shupela; 3-15-1926; 6 m; m; yes; F; Lobar pneumonia; yes

QUMAHEFTEWA, *(Blank)*; 3-11-1926; Very old; m; yes; F; Heart disease; yes

SEKIEONGEWA, Timothy; 1-30-1926; 13 yr; m; yes; F; Tubercular meningitis; yes

SEYOWNIM, *(Blank)*; 1-16-1926; 73 yr; f; yes; F; Pneumonia; yes

DEATHS, (Occurring between July 1, 1925, and June 30, 1926)

KEY: Year; and Number on Last Census Roll (if given); Name; Date of Death; Age at Death; Sex; Tribe (Hopi, unless otherwise indicated); Ward [yes or no]; Degree of Blood; Cause of Death; At jurisdiction where enrolled [yes or no]; (If "no", where?).

SEKIWINCIE, Lola; 6-14-1926; 8 yr; f; yes; F; Broken sorofula (scrofula) gland; yes

SOANEWA, Bertha; 6-16-1926; 6 d; f; yes; F; Premature baby; yes

TALASHMANEWA, Douglas; 3-14-1926; 48 yr; m; yes; F; Lobar pneumonia; yes

TALASSHO, *(Blank)*; 1-24-1926; 3 d; m; yes; F; Premature birth; yes

TALASYAMSE, Flora; 4-5-1926; 23 yr; f; yes; F; TB of lungs; yes

TALASYESEA, Welden; 3-14-1926; 8 m; m; yes; F; Croupous pneumonia; yes

TALAYUMPTEWA, Royal; 1-31-1926; 1 yr; m; yes; F; Inanition; yes

(No name); 5-1-1926; ?; f; yes; F; Blue baby; yes
Child of Kitty Keomongvisie

(No name); 4-6-1926; ?; m; yes; F; Stillborn; yes
Child of Henry Martin Uyoungwa

149

Index

153

Index

Index

www.ingramcontent.com/pod-product-compliance
Lightning Source LLC
Chambersburg PA
CBHW020254030426
42336CB00010B/754